T0224949

Building Native Web Components

Front-End Development with Polymer and Vue.js

Carlos Rojas

Apress®

Building Native Web Components: Front-End Development with Polymer and Vue.js

Carlos Rojas
Medellin, Colombia

ISBN-13 (pbk): 978-1-4842-5904-7   ISBN-13 (electronic): 978-1-4842-5905-4
https://doi.org/10.1007/978-1-4842-5905-4

Managing Director: Apress Media LLC: Welmoed Spahr
Acquisitions Editor: Spandana Chatterjee
Development Editor: Rita Fernando
Coordinating Editor: Shrikant Vishwakarma

Cover designed by eStudioCalamar

Cover image designed by Pexels

Distributed to the book trade worldwide by Springer Science+Business Media LLC, 1 New York Plaza, Suite 4600, New York, NY 10004. Phone 1-800-SPRINGER, fax (201) 348-4505, e-mail orders-ny@springer-sbm.com, or visit www.springeronline.com. Apress Media, LLC is a California LLC and the sole member (owner) is Springer Science+Business Media Finance Inc (SSBM Finance Inc). SSBM Finance Inc is a **Delaware** corporation.

For information on translations, please e-mail booktranslations@springernature.com; for reprint, paperback, or audio rights, please e-mail bookpermissions@springernature.com.

Apress titles may be purchased in bulk for academic, corporate, or promotional use. eBook versions and licenses are also available for most titles. For more information, reference our Print and eBook Bulk Sales web page at www.apress.com/bulk-sales.

Any source code or other supplementary material referenced by the author in this book is available to readers on GitHub via the book's product page, located at www.apress.com/978-1-4842-5904-7. For more detailed information, please visit www.apress.com/source-code.

Printed on acid-free paper

To my grandmothers, who always believed in me

Table of Contents

About the Author

Carlos Rojas is an engineer with more than ten years of experience building digital products. He is focused on front-end technologies (HTML, CSS, JS, Angular, React, Polymer, and Vue.js) and cutting-edge web technologies, such as Web Components, WebXR, and Progressive Web Apps. He also has experience working with Fortune 500 companies and fast-changing business environments, such as startups.

He enjoys sharing knowledge through talks at meetups, videos on YouTube, other books published by Apress, his personal blog (`https://medium.com/@carlosrojas_o`), and helping startups and other companies run workflows to make excellent digital products. As such, his books aim to convey his love for the construction of scalable, high-quality products.

About the Technical Reviewer

Yogendra Sharma is a developer with experience in architecture, design, and development of scalable and distributed applications, with a core interest in microservices and Spring. Currently, he works as an IoT and cloud architect at Intelizign Engineering Services Pvt, Pune.

Yogendra also has hands-on experience in such technologies as AWS, IoT, Python, J2SE, J2EE, NodeJS, Vue.js, Angular, MongoDB, and Docker. He is constantly exploring technical novelties and is open-minded and eager to learn about new technologies and frameworks. He has reviewed several books and video courses published by Apress and Packt.

Acknowledgments

To my friends, because they always found time to review my code and drafts; to my colleagues, because they helped me a lot with their feedback; to Yogendra, because his attention to detail made this book better; and to my editors, because their feedback and reviews have made this book a high-quality guide.

Introduction

Web Components are everywhere in the current front-end environment. The three most popular frameworks, Angular, React, and Vue.js, use Web Components as an architectural element. In this book, you will learn how to empower a web app, building small pieces that can be integrated into any modern JavaScript project and modified for future use, if your company decides to migrate its current web app to a new and more promising framework.

In Chapter 1, you will create your first native web component. I am going to guide you through all the steps that you require to create a placeholder component, using web platform specifications.

Chapter 2 covers the `CustomElement` specification. You will learn to use it to create custom tags on the Web and how its life cycle works.

Chapter 3 covers HTML templates. I will discuss the `<template>` and `<slot>` elements and how to build a component with these.

In Chapter 4, you will learn the Shadow DOM specification, how to add it in native Web Components, and what its benefits are.

Chapter 5 discusses ES modules specifications, how to create modules, and how to use modules in our web applications.

In Chapter 6, you will learn how to design components and make them work together in a web application. We will connect our web application to an API and define a dataflow for our components.

In Chapter 7, you will learn how to make our Web Components available in npm. You also will learn about browser support for Web Components APIS, how to add polyfills to support more web browsers, and how to add Webpack and Babel to process and prepare our Web Components for publication.

Chapter 8 covers how to build Web Components with Polymer, why Polymer is used instead of VanillaJS, how to use `LitElement` in our Web Components, and how to use `lit-html`.

In Chapter 9, we will develop an app. You will learn some key concepts and understand how to integrate Web Components and Vue.js.

In Chapter 10, you will see how Firebase hosting and Firebase authentication are used to release our final web app to the world.

CHAPTER 1

Making Your First Web Component

Welcome to building your first web component. This chapter discusses the various tools, technologies, designs, and development concepts that you will require to create your first web component. You will learn what a web component is, as well as what web browser support, design systems, and component-driven development (CDD) are.

What Are Web Components?

At a high level, Web Components are isolated pieces (kinds of blocks) with which a user interface (UI) can communicate with other elements, through properties and events (inputs and outputs from these blocks). Take the `<video>` element, for example. We can use this element with any technologies in a browser, and we can pass such properties as `width` and `height` and listen for events such as `onclick`.

In stricter terms, we can say that Web Components are a set of web platform APIs (application programming interfaces) that allow us to build HTML tags that will work across modern web browsers and can be used with any JavaScript technology (React, Angular, Vue.js, etc.).

Web Components have four main specifications:

- Custom elements

- Shadow DOM

- ES modules

- HTML templates

I will cover these specifications in greater depth in the next chapters.

1

C. Rojas, *Building Native Web Components*, https://doi.org/10.1007/978-1-4842-5905-4_1

History of Web Components

Currently, Web Components are everywhere in the front-end environment. The three most popular frameworks (Angular, React, and Vue.js) use Web Components as part of their architecture. It was not always so. Web Components were developed little by little over time. The first significant progress was achieved in 2010 with AngularJS (`https://angularjs.org`), which was a framework that introduced the concept of directives as a way to create your own tags, with their own features to build UIs. Later, in 2011, Alex Russell delivered a speech at a Fronteers Conference, titled "Web Components and Model Driven Views," that set out some key concepts and ideas that are now commonly used.[1] In 2013, Google took another big step forward with Polymer, a library based on Web Components (using web APIs) that has become a tool for building libraries, tools, and standards for a better Web.

Why Use Web Components?

Today, all front-end developers face two significant problems that can be a drain on companies' energy, time, and finances. These are as follows.

Legacy

Legacy, a well-known problem in software development, refers to an old code base that must be updated at some point, in order to operate with new JavaScript projects and tools.

Framework Churn

JavaScript's tools and its frameworks ecosystem are changing rapidly. It can be stressful and exhausting to choose the correct framework for a new project, because we can't guess for how long the framework will be relevant. This problem of relevance and how it affects investment in training and development for a set of tools that can quickly become obsolete is called framework churn.

---

[1]Alex Russell, "Web Components and Model Driven Views," *Fronteers* `https://fronteers.nl/ congres/2011/sessions/web-components-and-model-driven-views-alex-russell`, Accessed September 28, 2020.

Remember that Web Components are a set of web platform specifications. Therefore, they are something likely to be used in web browsers for a long time and offer many benefits, including the following:

- Web Components are reusable and work between frameworks.

- Web Components can run in all major web browsers.

- Web Components are easily maintainable and are prepared for the future, mainly because they are based in web platform specifications.

Basic Concepts of the Web Components Ecosystem

Throughout this book, I will be using several terms that are related to techniques, methodologies, or patterns that we can apply when using Web Components in our web apps. These are as follows.

Design Systems

Design systems are catalogs or collections of reusable components, guidelines, and tools that allow teams in organizations to build digital products to work more efficiently and apply consistent branding for all their products. Some examples with this approach are as follows:

- *Google*: Material Design (`https://material.io`)

- *Adobe*: Spectrum (`https://spectrum.adobe.com`)

- *Ionic*: Ionic Framework (`https://ionicframework.com/docs`)

Component-Driven Development

Component-driven development means designing your software applications by building independent components. Each component has an interface or API to communicate with the rest of the system. Some advantages of using this approach are

- *Faster development*: Separating development into components allows you to build modular parts with small scopes and small objectives. This means that you can develop faster and make a piece for testing available more quickly for reuse in some other system.

3

- *More straightforward maintenance*: When you must add or update the functionality of your application, you only have to update the component, instead of having to refactor more significant parts of your application.

- *Reusability*: Modular components allow for reusable functionality and can be extended to build multiple applications, eliminating the need to rewrite them over and over again.

- *Test-driven development (TDD)*: Implementing unit tests to validate the focused functionality of each modular component becomes much easier.

- *A better understanding of the system*: When a system is composed of modular components, it becomes easier to grasp, understand, and operate.

Browser Support for Web Components

At the time of writing (early 2020), Web Components are supported by all major web browsers (see Figure 1-1).

Figure 1-1. *Major browsers supporting the main specifications of Web Components*

Getting Started

To start to build apps with Web Components, you must understand and install several technologies and tools.

cmder (Windows Only)

cmder is a terminal emulator for Windows. By default, Windows operating systems come with a terminal (command prompt) that is not useful for development. That is why we need cmder, which is an emulator we can use to run commands smoothly in our terminal.

To access this emulator, go to cmder.net and download the latest version.

Extract the file in your C:/ location.

Go to System Properties ➤ Environment Variables and edit Path Variable, as in Figure 1-2.

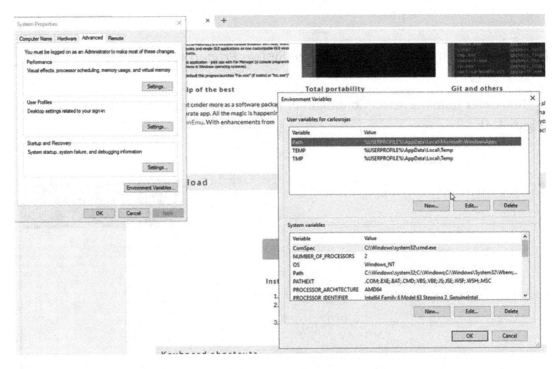

Figure 1-2. *Environment Variables preferences in System Properties*

Add the cmder location to the Path variable, as in Figure 1-3.

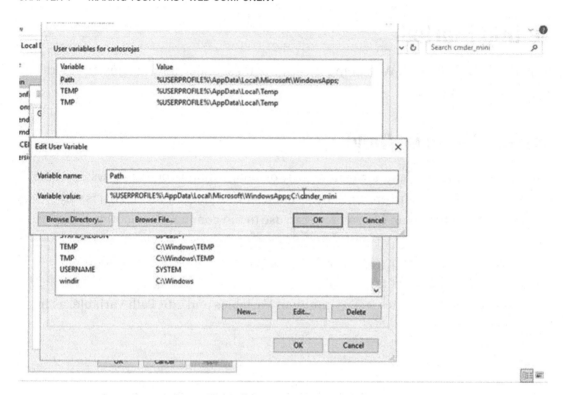

Figure 1-3. Path *variable preferences in System Properties*

Run cmder from the Select Command Prompt, to test the environment variable (Figure 1-4).

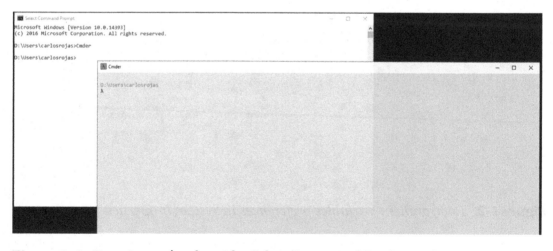

Figure 1-4. *Running* cmder *from the Select Command Prompt*

Node.js

Node.js is a JavaScript runtime environment. Most projects that use JavaScript use Node to install dependencies and create scripts to automate the development workflow.

You must install Node in your machine. You can download it from `https://nodejs.org/en/`.

Once you download the installer, run it and follow the instructions.

For Mac

If you are using a Mac, follow the installer instructions for Node.js shown in Figure 1-5.

Figure 1-5. *Node.js Mac installation*

Then open your terminal and run $node -v. If everything is OK, you will see the Node version in your terminal, as in Figure 1-6.

```
Last login: Wed Aug 19 10:54:59 on console
carlosrojaso@Carloss-MacBook-Pro-2 ~ % node -v
v10.16.3
carlosrojaso@Carloss-MacBook-Pro-2 ~ %
```

Figure 1-6. *Node version in the terminal*

For Windows

To install Node.js for Windows, follow the installer instructions shown in Figure 1-7.

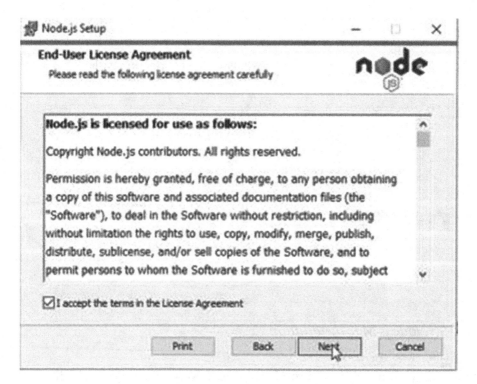

Figure 1-7. *Node.js Windows installation*

Then, when you finish, open cmder and run $ node -v.

npm

When you install Node.js, you install npm too. npm is a package manager for Node.js that allows users to install dependencies and run small scripts in their JavaScript projects.

For Mac and Windows

Check the npm version running in your terminal via $ npm -v. If everything is OK, you will see the npm version in your terminal, as in Figure 1-8.

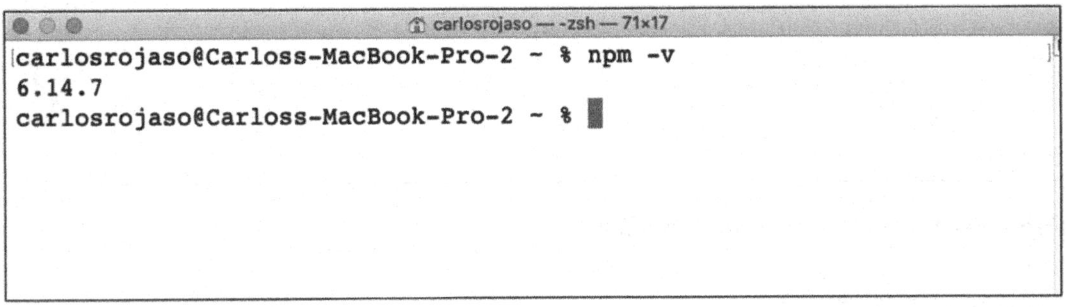

Figure 1-8. *npm version in the terminal*

Google Chrome

Chrome is a web browser that offers excellent support to Web Components and includes Chrome DevTools, a handy feature for developers. You can download and install Chrome from www.google.com/chrome/.

For Mac and Windows

To install Chrome for Mac and Windows, run the installer and follow the relevant steps. Once Chrome is successfully installed, open it, and you'll see a welcome screen (Figure 1-9).

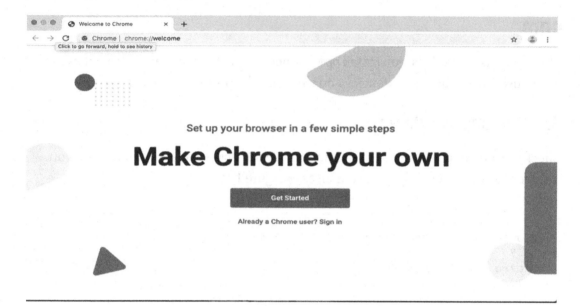

Figure 1-9. *Google Chrome installation*

Chrome DevTools

Chrome DevTools is a set of web developer tools included in the Google Chrome browser. This tool helps you as a developer to diagnose problems in your app and make it faster. To open, press Command+Option+J (Mac) or Control+Shift+J (Windows, Linux, Chrome OS), to jump straight into the console panel (Figure 1-10).

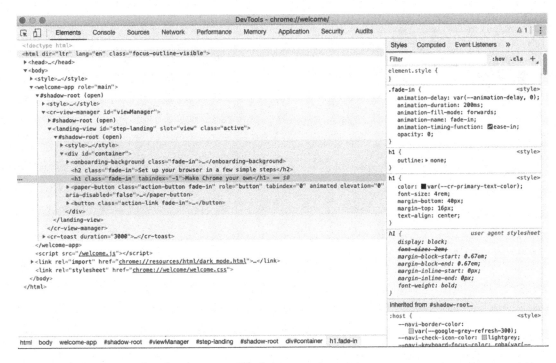

Figure 1-10. *Google Chrome DevTools*

Lighthouse

Lighthouse is an open source automated tool for improving the quality of web pages. Lighthouse can be found in Chrome's DevTools.[2] Go to the Audit tab to access it (Figure 1-11).

---

[2]Google Developers, "Lighthouse," https://developers.google.com/web/tools/lighthouse/, Accessed September 28, 2020.

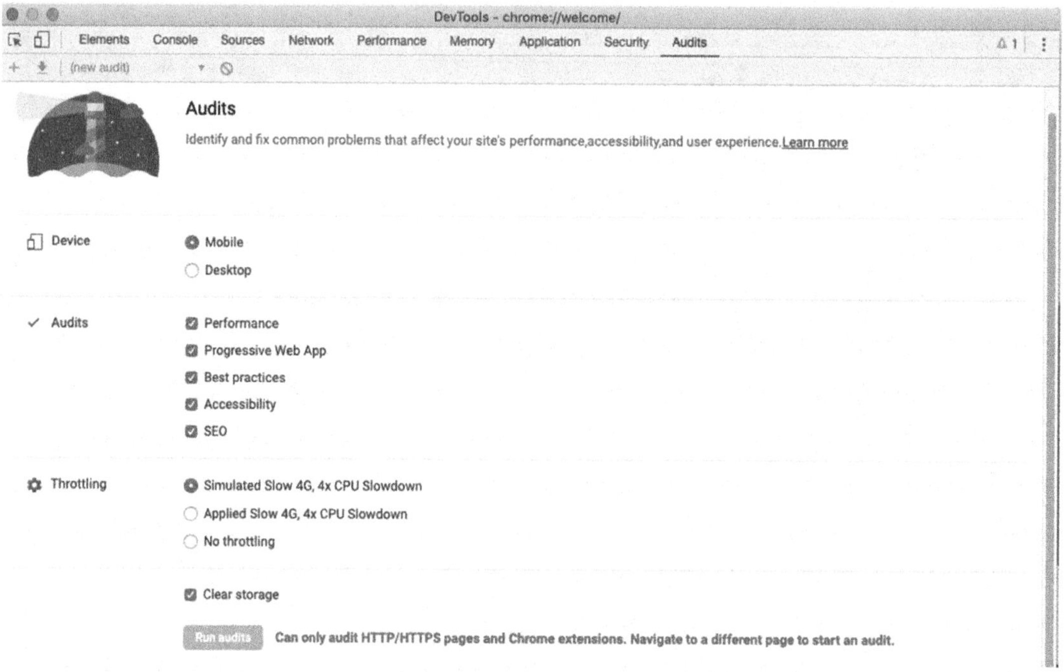

Figure 1-11. *Google Chrome DevTools Audits tab*

Vue

Some examples in this book will use the Vue.js framework. Vue.js is a straightforward and refreshing framework for JavaScript. Vue is oriented in the view layer mainly, but you can add what you require and build powerful progressive web applications with all the tools that are part of its ecosystem.

Using Vue in your project is really easy. You only have to add the following in your index.html, as in Listing 1-1.

Listing 1-1. Adding Vue from the cdn Development Version

```
<!-- development version, includes helpful console warnings -->
<script src="https://cdn.jsdelivr.net/npm/vue/dist/vue.js"></script>
```

Or adding the product version, as you see in Listing 1-2.

Listing 1-2. Adding Vue from the cdn Production Version

```
<!-- production version, optimized for size and speed -->
<script src="https://cdn.jsdelivr.net/npm/vue"></script>
```

Vue CLI

Vue CLI is a full system for rapid Vue.js development. Thanks to this tool, we can avoid some extra work when dealing with Webpack, EsLint, and other tools and focus on building business logic in our apps. You must install it in your system by running the following in your terminal: $npm install -g @vue/cli.

If everything is OK, you will see the Vue CLI version in your terminal, as in Figure 1-12.

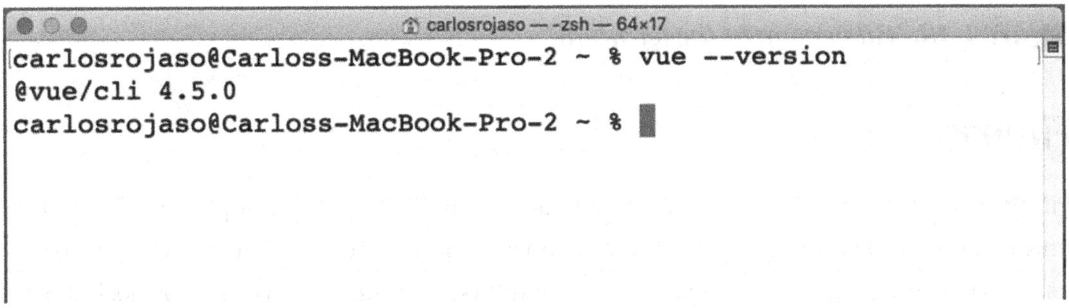

```
carlosrojaso@Carloss-MacBook-Pro-2 ~ % vue --version
@vue/cli 4.5.0
carlosrojaso@Carloss-MacBook-Pro-2 ~ %
```

Figure 1-12. *Vue CLI version in the terminal*

Git

Git is a version-control system designed to handle the different changes in our projects. We are going to use Git to manipulate our web app project and handle the successive steps outlined in each chapter. You can download and install Git from https://git-scm.com/downloads.

For Mac and Windows

To install, run the installer and follow the steps. When you finish, open cmder/terminal and run $ git -version.

If everything is OK, you will see the Git version in your terminal, as in Figure 1-13.

```
● ● ●                        ⌂ carlosrojaso — -zsh — 64×17
carlosrojaso@Carloss-MacBook-Pro-2 ~ % git --version
git version 2.24.3 (Apple Git-128)
carlosrojaso@Carloss-MacBook-Pro-2 ~ % ▮
```

Figure 1-13. *Git version in the terminal*

Firebase

Firebase is a cloud service that helps you to automate back-end development. You can understand Firebase as a place where you can save data, assets, and authenticate your users, without having back-end knowledge. Firebase is robust, and Google backs it. For our project, you must install the Firebase CLI in your terminal, via $npm install -g firebase-tools.

Additionally, you must sign up at https://firebase.google.com/ and create a new project. I created the project "apress-book-webcomponents" (Figure 1-14). I will use this project to connect and publish all the features covered in this book.

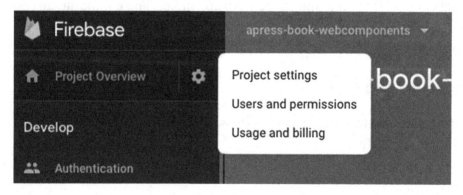

Figure 1-14. *Firebase web console Project Overview*

Throughout this book, we are going to use Authentication, Database, and Hosting to empower our app.

Firebase Authentication

Firebase Authentication is the service that allows us to have an authentication system in our app, to handle security and server-related issues.

You can access Firebase Authentication from your web console (`https://console.firebase.google.com`) via Develop ➤ Authentication (Figure 1-15).

Figure 1-15. *Firebase web console Authentication*

Firebase Database

Firebase Database is a service with which we can add a remote database that is going to keep our user data. In addition, it is an excellent option for handling real-time in our app, which means that we can open our app from either a mobile or desktop device, and the same information will be shown.

You can find Firebase Database from your web console (`https://console.firebase.google.com`) in Develop ➤ Database (Figure 1-16).

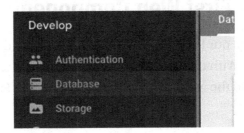

Figure 1-16. *Firebase web console Database*

Firebase Hosting

Firebase Hosting is a hosting service with which you can serve all your static files, connect your domain, and get an SSL Certificate quickly. It is also easy to deploy.

You can find Firebase Hosting from your web console (`https://console.firebase.google.com`) via Develop ➤ Hosting (Figure 1-17).

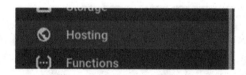

Figure 1-17. *Firebase web console Hosting*

Visual Studio Code

Visual Studio Code is a free code editor that assists development with a pack of integrated tools and the possibility of extending them through plug-ins. You can download Visual Studio Code from `https://code.visualstudio.com/`.

For Mac and Windows

To install Visual Studio Code, just run the installer and follow the steps. Then open Visual Studio Code from your Applications/Programs list.

Numerous code editors are available, but we are going to use Visual Studio Code in this book mainly because it is free, works smoothly, and has a big plug-in ecosystem.

Developing Our First Web Component

Now we are going to create our first web component, a placeholder we'll call `vanilla-placeholder-component`. With this component, you can fill blocks on your web page with a red background and the word "placeholder," as shown in Figure 1-18.

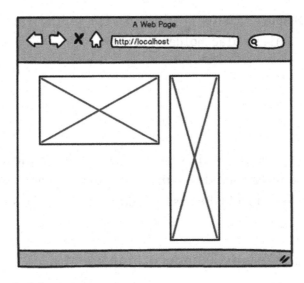

Figure 1-18. *Placeholder component*

The basic usage of this component in our HTML is as in Listing 1-3.

Listing 1-3. Using `vanilla-placeholder-component`

```
<vanilla-placeholder-content></vanilla-placeholder-content>
```

We can add some attributes, as in Listing 1-4.

Listing 1-4. Using `vanilla-placeholder-component` with Attributes

```
<vanilla-placeholder-content height="100px" width="50px">
</vanilla-placeholder-content>
```

Our component accepts height and width properties to customize the size, but if we don't provide that info, we are going to assign 100px by default for both.

First we must create a file `index.html` and fill it with a basic structure, as shown in Listing 1-5.

Listing 1-5. `index.html`—Basic Structure

```
<!DOCTYPE html>
<html lang="en">
<head>
    <meta charset="UTF-8">
```

17

```
    <meta name="viewport" content="width=device-width, initial-scale=1.0">
    <title>Demo - vanilla-placeholder</title>
</head>
<body>
</body>
</html>
```

With this code, we have a basic HTML page with nothing in the body. Therefore, we are going to add some JavaScript with the `<script></script>` tags before the `</body>`, and we are going to add the basic structure to create a custom component, as in Listing 1-6.

Listing 1-6. Adding a Custom Component in `index.html`

```
<!DOCTYPE html>
<html lang="en">
<head>
    <meta charset="UTF-8">
    <meta name="viewport" content="width=device-width, initial-scale=1.0">
    <title>Demo - vanilla-placeholder</title>
</head>
<body>
<script>
class VanillaPlaceholderContent extends HTMLElement {
    constructor() {}
}
customElements.define('vanilla-placeholder-content',
VanillaPlaceholderContent);
</script>
</body>
</html>
```

With this, we are going to define our tag `<vanilla-placeholder-content>` and create a JavaScript class that inherits from HTMLElement (https://developer.mozilla.org/en-US/docs/Web/API/HTMLElement) and gives us the opportunity to define our component.

Finally, we will add some code to the VanillaPlaceholderContent class, as shown in Listing 1-7.

Listing 1-7. Adding Component Logic to vanilla-placeholder-component

```
<!DOCTYPE html>
<html lang="en">
<head>
    <meta charset="UTF-8">
    <meta name="viewport" content="width=device-width, initial-scale=1.0">
    <title>Demo - vanilla-placeholder</title>
</head>
<body>
<script>
class VanillaPlaceholderContent extends HTMLElement {

    constructor() {
        super();
        const placeholder = document.createElement('template');
        const height = this.getAttribute('height') || '100px';
        const width = this.getAttribute('width') || '100px';
        placeholder.innerHTML = VanillaPlaceholderContent.template
        (height, width);

        this.appendChild(document.importNode(placeholder.content, true));
    }

    static template (height, width) {
        return `
        <style>
        .placeholder {
            background-color: red;
            width: ${height};
            height: ${width};
        }
        </style>
        <div class='placeholder'>Placeholder</div>`;
    }
```

```
}
customElements.define('vanilla-placeholder-content',
VanillaPlaceholderContent);
</script>
</body>
</html>
```

In general terms, we are using the constructor() to initialize our component, and with this.getAttribute(''), we are checking if we are getting some properties, such as height and width. Following that, we are using the template() method to create our elements and the styling, and finally, we are using this.appendChild(document. importNode(placeholder.content, true)); to add that in our UI.

We can see the results in our web browser (Figure 1-19).

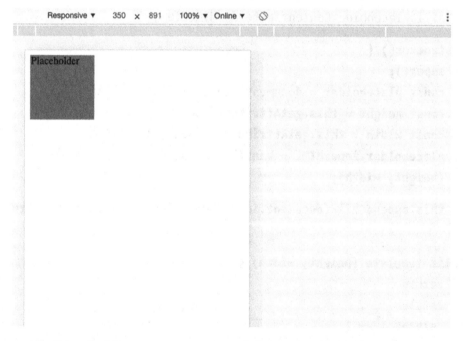

Figure 1-19. *Placeholder component in web browser*

Don't worry if some things are difficult to understand for now. In the following chapters, you are going to learn more about this API and why it is useful.

You can access the source code for this book (https://github.com/carlosrojaso/ apress-book-web-components) at $git checkout chap-1.

Summary

In this chapter, you learned the following:

- What Web Components are and what the current support in the major browsers is

- What a design system is and some examples that we can find on the Web

- What component-driven development (CDD) is and what the advantages of using this approach in our software applications are

CHAPTER 2

Custom Elements

In this chapter, we are going to explore the Custom Elements specification in the Web Components set. You will learn what custom elements are, how to create them, and what the life cycle for custom elements is. We are then going to build a new web component for our collection.

What Are Custom Elements?

Custom Elements is a mechanism that web developers can use to create new HTML tags. We can create our tags by using the `CustomElementRegistry` object. For example, we can define a `random-icon-placeholder`, as in Listing 2-1.

Listing 2-1. Defining a Web Component with `CustomElements`

```
class randomIconPlaceholder extends HTMLElement {
    constructor(){...}
}
customElements.define('random-icon-placeholder', randomIconPlaceholder);
```

Here, we are using a name that is in lowercase, separated by hyphens (kebab-case), which is required to assign a name to custom tags. In addition, we are using a class that is extending from `HTMLElement`. `HTMLElement` is the main object in HTML, and any element in the Document Object Model (DOM) will have inherited its properties. (You can find more information at `https://developer.mozilla.org/en-US/docs/Web/API/HTMLElement`.)

There are two types of custom elements: autonomous and customized. An autonomous custom element doesn't inherit from another standard HTML element, such as `<p>`, `<a>`, `<br>`, and so on. We can say that `<random-icon-placeholder>` in the previous example (Listing 2-1) is an autonomous custom element.

© Carlos Rojas 2021
C. Rojas, *Building Native Web Components*, https://doi.org/10.1007/978-1-4842-5905-4_2

Customized built-in elements inherit from another standard HTML element. For example, we can define one element that extends the `<p>` element, as in Listing 2-2.

Listing 2-2. Defining a Customized `CustomElement`

```
class randomParagraphSizePlaceholder extends HTMLParagraphElement {
    constructor(){...}
}

customElements.define('random-paragraph-size-placeholder',
randomParagraphSizePlaceholder, {extends: p});
```

Now we can use this element in our HTML document, as in Listing 2-3.

Listing 2-3. Using a Customized `CustomElement`

```
<p is="random-paragraph-size-placeholder">Some text</p>
```

You can find a list of interfaces to inherit at `https://html.spec.whatwg.org/multipage/indices.html#element-interfaces`.

Custom Elements' Life Cycle Hooks

When we define a custom element, we can use life cycle hooks to run code in specific moments during the component life in our component. There are four main moments in our custom element that we can use.

> `constructor`: This is triggered when an instance of the element is created or upgraded. It is useful for initializing variables, add event listeners, or creating a Shadow DOM.

> `connectedCallback`: This is triggered each time a custom element is appended into a document. This will occur each time the node is moved and may happen before the element's contents have been fully parsed.

attributeChangedCallback (attrName, oldVal, newVal): This is invoked each time one of the custom element's attributes is added, removed, or changed. The observed attributes to notice a change are specified with the static get observedAttributes method.

disconnectedCallback: This is invoked each time the custom element is disconnected from the document's DOM.

We can see all the preceding methods of the Web Components life cycle in Figure 2-1.

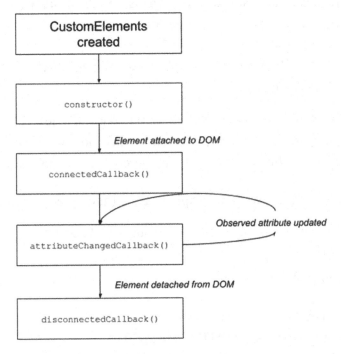

Figure 2-1. *Web Components life cycle*

Building a Custom Element

To learn how to use the customElements object and the life cycle hooks, we are going to create the randomParagraphSizePlaceholder component. This simple component generates a random number between 12 and 50px and receives the attribute 'text'.

To use this component in our HTML document, we must call <random-paragraph-size-placeholder>, as in Listing 2-4.

Listing 2-4. Using `random-paragraph-size-placeholder`

```
<random-paragraph-size-placeholder text="My Personal Text"></random-
paragraph-size-placeholder>
```

Next, we must create a generic structure for an autonomous custom element, as in Listing 2-5.

Listing 2-5. Declaring `random-paragraph-size-placeholder` Component

```
class RandomParagraphSizePlaceholder extends HTMLElement {
    constructor(){...}
}
customElements.define('random-paragraph-size-placeholder',
RandomParagraphSizePlaceholder);
```

With this, the web browser knows that we want to register a new HTML tag.

Later, we are going to add the life cycle hooks as methods, and we are going to add `console.log()`, to know when the method is triggered. (See Listing 2-6.)

Listing 2-6. Defining `random-paragraph-size-placeholder` Component

```
class RandomParagraphSizePlaceholder extends HTMLElement {
    constructor(){
      console.log(`contructor.`)
    }
    connectedCallback() {
        console.log(`connectedCallback hook`);
    }
    disconnectedCallback() {
        console.log(`disconnectedCallback hook`);
    }
 attributeChangedCallback(attrName, oldVal, newVal) {
        console.log(`attributeChangedCallback hook`);
    }
}
customElements.define('random-paragraph-size-placeholder',
RandomParagraphSizePlaceholder);
```

To get the `attributeChangedCallback()` method to work correctly, we must add the static method `observedAttributes()` and return the properties that we want to observe. In this case, we only have the `'text'` property, as in Listing 2-7.

Listing 2-7. Adding Text to Be Observed in `attributeChangedCallback`

```
static get observedAttributes() {
      return ['text'];
   }
```

Next, we'll add the basic logic in the constructor, to generate random numbers and send them to the `template` method, as in Listing 2-8.

Listing 2-8. Adding the Logic to Initialize `random-paragraph-size-placeholder`

```
constructor() {
        console.log(`constructor hook`);
        super();
        const placeholder = document.createElement('template');
        const myText = this.getAttribute('text') || 'Loren Ipsum';
        const randomSize = Math.floor((Math.random() * (50 - 12 + 1)) + 12);
        placeholder.innerHTML = RandomParagraphSizePlaceholder.template
        (myText, randomSize);
        this.appendChild(document.importNode(placeholder.content, true));
   }
```

Altogether, the code will look as shown in Listing 2-9.

Listing 2-9. Final Code for `random-paragraph-size-placeholder`

```
<!DOCTYPE html>
<html lang="en">
<head>
    <meta charset="UTF-8">
    <meta name="viewport" content="width=device-width, initial-scale=1.0">
    <title>Demo - random-paragraph-size-placeholder</title>
</head>
```

```html
<body>
<div id="parent">
    <random-paragraph-size-placeholder text="My Personal Text">
    </random-paragraph-size-placeholder>
</div>
<button id="myButton" onclick="removeElement()">Remove Element</button>
<script>
class RandomParagraphSizePlaceholder extends HTMLElement {

    constructor() {
        console.log(`constructor hook`);
        super();
        const placeholder = document.createElement('template');
        const myText = this.getAttribute('text') || 'Loren Ipsum';
        const randomSize = Math.floor((Math.random() * (50 - 12 + 1)) + 12);
        placeholder.innerHTML = RandomParagraphSizePlaceholder.
        template(myText, randomSize);

        this.appendChild(document.importNode(placeholder.content, true));
    }

    static get observedAttributes() {
        return ['text'];
    }

    set text(val) {
        if (val) {
            this.setAttribute(`text`, val);
        } else {
            this.setAttribute(`text`, ``);
        }
    }

    get text() {
        return this.getAttribute('text');
    }
```

```
    connectedCallback() {
        console.log(`connectedCallback hook`);
    }
    disconnectedCallback() {
        console.log(`disconnectedCallback hook`);
    }

    attributeChangedCallback(attrName, oldVal, newVal) {
        console.log(`attributeChangedCallback hook`);
        console.log(`attrName`, attrName);
        console.log(`oldVal`, oldVal);
        console.log(`newVal`, newVal);
    }

    static template (myText, randomSize) {
        return `
        <div style="font-size:${randomSize}px">${myText}</div>`;
    }
}
customElements.define('random-paragraph-size-placeholder',
RandomParagraphSizePlaceholder);

const element = document.querySelector('random-paragraph-size-placeholder');

function removeElement() {
    const parentElement = document.getElementById('parent')
    parentElement.removeChild(element);
    const myButton = document.getElementById('myButton');
    myButton.disabled = true;
}
</script>
</body>
</html>
```

You'll also notice that I've added an extra function, removeElement, to see how disconnectedCallback() is triggered when I remove the component from the DOM. You can access the code for this book (https://github.com/carlosrojaso/apress-book-web-components) at $git checkout chap-2.

Summary

In this chapter, you learned the following:

- What the `CustomElementRegistry` object is and how to use it

- What the two main types of custom elements are

- What life cycle hooks are and when they are triggered

CHAPTER 3

HTML Template

In this chapter, we are going to examine HTML Template, another specification in the Web Components set. You are going to learn what an HTML Template is and how to use HTML templates in web components. We then will build a new web component for our collection.

What Is an HTML Template?

The HTML Template specification defines the `<template>` element, to create fragments of markup to be unused in our custom element until we activate them later on runtime. These fragments can be cloned and inserted in HTML by script.

The content inside a `<template>` has the following properties:

- The content will not render until it is activated. The markup inside `<template>` is hidden and doesn't render.

- The content will not have side effects. The scripts, images, and media tags don't run until activated.

- The content will not be considered to be in the Document Object Model (DOM). Using `getElementById()` or `querySelector()` won't return child nodes of a template.

The basic way to use `<template>` is indicated in Listing 3-1.

Listing 3-1. Basic Example of Using `<template>`

```
<template id="my-error-message">
    <p>
        Some error messages.
    </p>
</template>
```

© Carlos Rojas 2021
C. Rojas, *Building Native Web Components*, https://doi.org/10.1007/978-1-4842-5905-4_3

My paragraph is hidden from the DOM, as shown in Figure 3-1.

```
<html>
<head>
</head>
<body>
      <img src='img.png'/>
      <p>Loren Ipsum</p>
      <template "my-error-message">
      <p> Error message </p>
      </template>
</body>
</html>
```

Rendered ──────────►

```
<html>
<head>
</head>
<body>
      <img/>
      <p>Loren Ipsum</p>
</body>
</html>
```

Code

Web page

Figure 3-1. *Hidden paragraph in a web page with a template*

If I want to show my content, I must activate it with code, as shown in Listing 3-2.

Listing 3-2. Activating Content in `<template>`

```
let myTemplate = document.getElementById('my-error-message');
let myContent = myTemplate.content;
document.body.appendChild(myContent);
```

In this way, we can activate the content in our document, as shown in Figure 3-2.

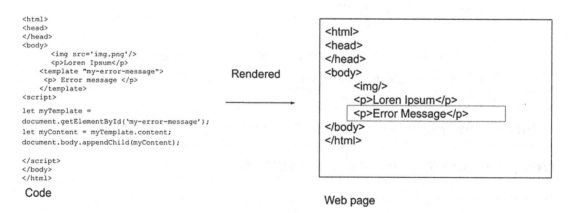

Figure 3-2. *Activating* template *in a web page*

Slots

In addition to <template>, we can take advantage of <slot> inside our content. Slots allow you to define placeholders in your template, as shown in Figure 3-3. Combined with other Web Components specifications, slots can be very useful in inserting markup inside elements.

The basic way to use <slot> is outlined in Listing 3-3.

Listing 3-3. Using <slot>

```
<p>
    <slot>This is a default message</slot>
</p>
```

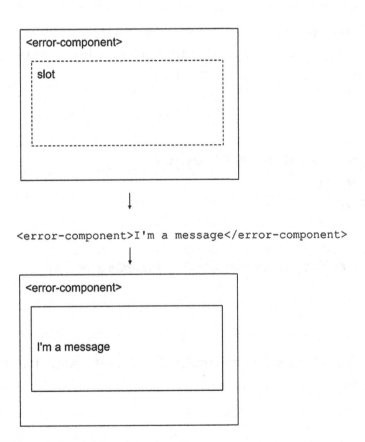

Figure 3-3. *Filling a slot with a message in* error-component

Building a Web Component with <template>

Now we are going to create a component to handle error and warning messages in our apps. With this component, you can send a kind of error or warning message, and the message that you want to show between <error-component></error-component>. If you are sending an error message, you will see the message against a red background. A warning message will be set against a yellow background.

First, we are going to create the basic structure for our component, as shown in Listing 3-4.

Listing 3-4. Basic Structure of error-component

```
<!DOCTYPE html>
<html lang="en">
<head>
    <meta charset="UTF-8">
    <meta name="viewport" content="width=device-width, initial-scale=1.0">
    <title>Demo - error-component</title>
</head>
<body>
<script>
class ErrorComponent extends HTMLElement {
    constructor() {
        super();
    }
}
customElements.define('error-component', ErrorComponent);
</script>
</body>
</html>
```

Now we are going to create the static method template(), with which we are going to generate our markup, as in Listing 3-5.

Listing 3-5. Adding the template() Method

```
<!DOCTYPE html>
<html lang="en">
<head>
    <meta charset="UTF-8">
    <meta name="viewport" content="width=device-width, initial-scale=1.0">
    <title>Demo - error-component</title>
</head>
<body>
<script>
class ErrorComponent extends HTMLElement {
    constructor() {
        super();
    }

    static template () {
        return `
        <template class="warning-type">
            <style>
                .warning {
                    background-color: yellow;
                    padding: 15px;
                    color: black;
                }
            </style>
            <div class="warning">
                <slot>Error component<slot>
            </div>
        </template>
        <template class="error-type">
            <style>
                .error {
                    background-color: red;
                    padding: 15px;
                    color: black;
                }
```

```
            </style>
            <div class="error">
                <slot>Error component<slot>
            </div>
        </template>
        <template class="none-type">
            <style>
                .none {
                    background-color: gray;
                    padding: 15px;
                    color: black;
                }
            </style>
            <div class="none">
                <slot>Error component<slot>
            </div>
        </template>
        `;
    }
}
customElements.define('error-component', ErrorComponent);
</script>
</body>
</html>
```

In our markup, we have three `<template>` blocks—one for each kind of message that we can receive: error, warning, and none. In addition, we are adding `<slot>` in each of these, which will take the value that we pass between our tags, as in Listing 3-6.

Listing 3-6. Passing Error Messages with Slots

```
<error-component>Value that the slot going to take</error-component>
```

Finally, we are going to use the life cycle hook `connectedCallback()` to handle the logic for choosing which template to use, as in Listing 3-7.

Listing 3-7. Initializing Properties in connectedCallback()

```
<!DOCTYPE html>
<html lang="en">
<head>
    <meta charset="UTF-8">
    <meta name="viewport" content="width=device-width, initial-scale=1.0">
    <title>Demo - error-component</title>
</head>
<body>
<script>
class ErrorComponent extends HTMLElement {
    constructor() {
        super();
    }

    connectedCallback() {
        this.root = this.attachShadow({mode: 'open'});
        this.templates = document.createElement('div');
        this.container = document.createElement('div');
        this.root.appendChild(this.templates);
        this.root.appendChild(this.container);
        this.templates.innerHTML = ErrorComponent.template();
        const kind = this.getAttribute(`kind`) || `none`;

        const template = this.templates.querySelector(`template.
        ${kind}-type`);
        if (template) {
            const clone = template.content.cloneNode(true);
            this.container.innerHTML = '';
            this.container.appendChild(clone);
        }
    }
```

```
static template () {
    return `
    <template class="warning-type">
        <style>
            .warning {
                background-color: yellow;
                padding: 15px;
                color: black;
            }
        </style>
        <div class="warning">
            <slot>Error component<slot>
        </div>
    </template>
    <template class="error-type">
        <style>
            .error {
                background-color: red;
                padding: 15px;
                color: black;
            }
        </style>
        <div class="error">
            <slot>Error component<slot>
        </div>
    </template>
    <template class="none-type">
        <style>
            .none {
                background-color: gray;
                padding: 15px;
                color: black;
            }
        </style>
```

```
        <div class="none">
            <slot>Error component<slot>
        </div>
    </template>
    `;
  }

}
customElements.define('error-component', ErrorComponent);
</script>
</body>
</html>
```

Here, we are using `'this'` to make references in our component, and we are using the method `connectedCallback()` to initialize these properties.

We are using the Shadow DOM `'this.attachShadow({mode: 'open'});'` as well. Shadow DOMs are the topic of the next chapter, but you can think of the one here as a protected DOM tree specific to our component.

In this logic, we are getting the `'kind'` attribute and rendering the correct `<template>`, whether it's an error, warning, or none. You can see the result in Figure 3-4.

Figure 3-4. *Using the error component on Chrome*

You can access the relevant code from the repo (`https://github.com/carlosrojaso/apress-book-web-components`) at `$git checkout chap-3`.

Summary

In this chapter, you learned the following:

- What `<template>` is and how to use it in our web components

- What `<slot>` is and how to use it in our web components

- How to create a web component to handle errors and warnings

CHAPTER 4

Shadow DOM

In this chapter, you are going to get acquainted with Shadow DOM, another specification in the set of Web Components. You will learn what Shadow DOM is and how to use it in web components. Next, we will build a new web component for our collection.

What Is Shadow DOM?

The Shadow DOM specification defines a mechanism with which to encapsulate our web components. The markup and styles that we create inside our web components protect it from external DOM manipulation and lobal CSS rules.

Consider, for example, the HTML 5 `<video>` tag. If we want a video player in our document, we create something similar to what is shown in Listing 4-1.

Listing 4-1. Using `video tag`

```
<video width="640" height="480" controls>
  <source src="myVideo.mp4" type="video/mp4">
  Your browser does not support the video tag.
</video>
```

However, when you view what is rendered in the web browser (Figure 4-1), you can see a complex combination of CSS styles, divs, and inputs that are encapsulated for the external modifications, and you only can see the tag `<video>`. That is the power of Shadow DOM.

© Carlos Rojas 2021
C. Rojas, *Building Native Web Components*, https://doi.org/10.1007/978-1-4842-5905-4_4

Figure 4-1. `<video>` *tag in Google Chrome*

Following are some benefits of Shadow DOM:

- Shadow DOM creates an isolated DOM that allows us to manipulate the DOM in our web components without worrying about external nodes.

- Shadow DOM creates a scoped CSS, which means that we can create more generic rules and not worry about naming conflicts.

The fundamental way to use Shadow DOM is shown in Listing 4-2. You may remember that we used this method in Chapter 3, when in Listing 3-7, we added a Shadow DOM to our web component, to activate/deactivate the templates in our example.

Listing 4-2. Attaching a Shadow DOM

```
let shadowElement = element.attachShadow({mode: 'open'});
```

The `attachShadow()` in the preceding code snippet receives a mode that can be `'open'` or `'closed'`. `'open'` means that you can access the Shadow DOM from the main context, and `'closed'` means that you can't.

Shadow Root

The Shadow root is the root node in the DOM created by our Shadow DOM (Figure 4-2).

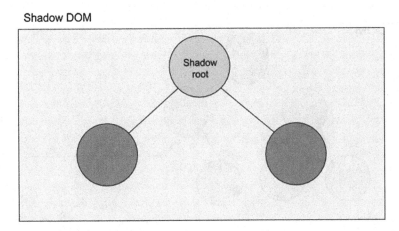

Figure 4-2. *Shadow root node in the Shadow DOM*

Shadow Tree

The Shadow tree is the DOM tree created by our Shadow DOM (Figure 4-3).

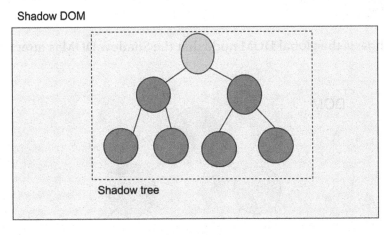

Figure 4-3. *Shadow tree in the Shadow DOM*

Shadow Boundary

The limit where our Shadow DOM ends and the global DOM continues (Figure 4-4) is the Shadow boundary.

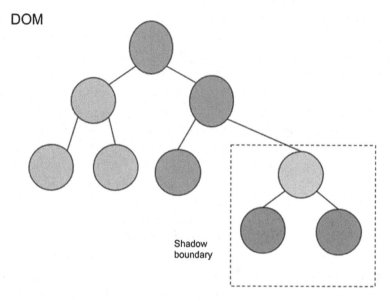

Figure 4-4. *Shadow boundary in our web app DOM*

Shadow Host

The Shadow host is the global DOM node that the Shadow DOM is attached to (Figure 4-5).

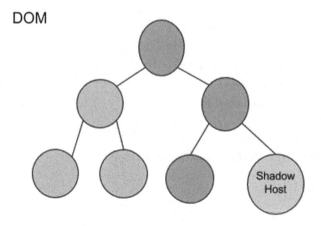

Figure 4-5. *Shadow host in our web app DOM*

Building SocialShareComponent

To use Shadow DOM, we are going to build a simple component, called `<social-share-component>`, to add social networks links to our apps. This component receives two parameters, `'socialNetwork'` and `'user'`, in which `'tw'` means Twitter and `'fb'` means Facebook. First, we are going to define our component, as shown in Listing 4-3.

Listing 4-3. Defining SocialShareComponent

```
class SocialShareComponent extends HTMLElement {}
customElements.define('social-share-component', SocialShareComponent);
```

Next, we are going to define some getters and setters in our component, to handle the `'socialNetwork'` and `'user'` parameters, as in Listing 4-4.

Listing 4-4. Defining SocialShareComponent

```
class SocialShareComponent extends HTMLElement {

    get socialNetwork() {
        return this.getAttribute('socialNetwork') || 'tw';
    }

    set socialNetwork(newValue) {
        this.setAttribute('socialNetwork', newValue);
    }

    get user() {
        return this.getAttribute('user') || 'none';
    }

    set user(newValue) {
        this.setAttribute('user', newValue);
    }
}
customElements.define('social-share-component', SocialShareComponent);
```

Also, we are going to define some static methods, to add markup and styles to our components, as shown in Listing 4-5.

Listing 4-5. Static Methods to Add Markup and Styles

```
class SocialShareComponent extends HTMLElement {

    get socialNetwork() {
        return this.getAttribute('socialNetwork') || 'tw';
    }

    set socialNetwork(newValue) {
        this.setAttribute('socialNetwork', newValue);
    }

    get user() {
        return this.getAttribute('user') || 'none';
    }

    set user(newValue) {
        this.setAttribute('user', newValue);
    }

    static twTemplate(user) {
        return `
        ${SocialShareComponent.twStyle()}
        <span class="twitter-button">
            <a href="https://twitter.com/${user}">
                Follow @${user}
            </a>
        </span>`;
    }

    static twStyle() {
        return `
        <style>
        a {
            height: 20px;
            padding: 3px 6px;
            background-color: #1b95e0;
            color: #fff;
            border-radius: 3px;
```

```
            font-weight: 500;
            font-size: 11px;
            font-family:'Helvetica Neue', Arial, sans-serif;
            line-height: 18px;
            text-decoration: none;
        }

        a:hover {  background-color: #0c7abf; }

        span {
            margin: 5px 2px;
        }
        </style>`;
    }

    static fbTemplate(user) {
        return `
        ${SocialShareComponent.fbStyle()}
        <span class="facebook-button">
            <a href="https://facebook.com/${user}">
                Follow @${user}
            </a>
        </span>`;
    }

    static fbStyle() {
        return `
        <style>
        a {
            height: 20px;
            padding: 3px 6px;
            background-color: #4267b2;
            color: #fff;
            border-radius: 3px;
            font-weight: 500;
            font-size: 11px;
            font-family:'Helvetica Neue', Arial, sans-serif;
```

```
            line-height: 18px;
            text-decoration: none;
        }

        a:hover {   background-color: #0c7abf; }

        span {
            margin: 5px 2px;
        }
        </style>`;
    }
}
customElements.define('social-share-component', SocialShareComponent);
```

Finally, we are going to build our constructor() method, as in Listing 4-6, with which we are going to attach the Shadow DOM in the root of our component and append to this a div element that is going to work as a container for our markup and styles.

Listing 4-6. Adding a constructor() in SocialShareComponent

```
class SocialShareComponent extends HTMLElement {

    constructor() {
        super();

        this.root = this.attachShadow({mode: 'open'});
        this.container = document.createElement('div');
        this.root.appendChild(this.container);

        switch(this.socialNetwork) {
            case 'tw':
                this.container.innerHTML = SocialShareComponent.twTemplate
                (this.user);
                break;
            case 'fb':
                this.container.innerHTML = SocialShareComponent.
                fbTemplate(this.user);
                break;
        }
    }
```

```
get socialNetwork() {
    return this.getAttribute('socialNetwork') || 'tw';
}

set socialNetwork(newValue) {
    this.setAttribute('socialNetwork', newValue);
}

get user() {
    return this.getAttribute('user') || 'none';
}

set user(newValue) {
    this.setAttribute('user', newValue);
}

static twTemplate(user) {
    return `
    ${SocialShareComponent.twStyle()}
    <span class="twitter-button">
        <a href="https://twitter.com/${user}">
            Follow @${user}
        </a>
    </span>`;
}

static twStyle() {
    return `
    <style>
    a {
        height: 20px;
        padding: 3px 6px;
        background-color: #1b95e0;
        color: #fff;
        border-radius: 3px;
        font-weight: 500;
        font-size: 11px;
        font-family:'Helvetica Neue', Arial, sans-serif;
```

```
        line-height: 18px;
        text-decoration: none;
    }

    a:hover {  background-color: #0c7abf; }

    span {
        margin: 5px 2px;
    }
    </style>`;
}

static fbTemplate(user) {
    return `
    ${SocialShareComponent.fbStyle()}
    <span class="facebook-button">
        <a href="https://facebook.com/${user}">
            Follow @${user}
        </a>
    </span>`;
}

static fbStyle() {
    return `
    <style>
    a {
        height: 20px;
        padding: 3px 6px;
        background-color: #4267b2;
        color: #fff;
        border-radius: 3px;
        font-weight: 500;
        font-size: 11px;
        font-family:'Helvetica Neue', Arial, sans-serif;
        line-height: 18px;
        text-decoration: none;
    }
```

```
a:hover {  background-color: #0c7abf; }

span {
    margin: 5px 2px;
}
</style>`;
  }
}
customElements.define('social-share-component', SocialShareComponent);
```

Here we are using switch() to handle what markup and styles we need to use, depending on the 'socialNetwork' parameter. The result is shown in Figure 4-6.

Figure 4-6. *Using social-share-component in Google Chrome*

You can access the code for this book (https://github.com/carlosrojaso/apress-book-web-components) at $git checkout chap-4.

Summary

In this chapter, you learned the following:

- What Shadow DOM is and how to use it in our web components

- What Shadow root, Shadow tree, Shadow boundary, and Shadow host are

- How to use Shadow DOM to create a web component to add social networks in our web apps

CHAPTER 5

ES Modules

In this chapter, I will discuss ES Modules, another specification in the Web Components set. You will learn what ES Modules are and how to use ES Modules in web components. We will then build a new web component for our collection.

What Are ES Modules?

The ES Modules specification defines a mechanism with which to share variables and functions in our projects through different files. ES Modules are now available with ES6. Before this, if you wanted to share something, you would add it to the global context and make it available whether it was used or not. Consider the code in Listing 5-1.

Listing 5-1. Using Constants in `main.js`

```
var pi = 3.1415;
var euler = 2.7182;

function getCircumference(radius) {
  return 2 * pi * radius;
}

function getCalcOneYear(interestRate, currentVal) {
  return currentVal * (euler ** interestRate);
}

console.log(getCircumference(2)); // 12.566
console.log(getCalcOneYear(0.3, 100)); // 134. 98466170045035
```

In `main.js`, we have two values, `pi` and `euler`, that are required in the functions `getCircumference` and `getCalcOneYear`. But what if we require `pi` and `euler` in different functions in different places in our application?

53

© Carlos Rojas 2021
C. Rojas, *Building Native Web Components*, https://doi.org/10.1007/978-1-4842-5905-4_5

To make it easier to share these values, we can create a new file, `math-constants.js`, and, using `'export'`, tell JavaScript that we are available to import that value. This is shown in Listing 5-2.

Listing 5-2. Exporting Values in file `math-constants.js`

```
export const pi = 3.1415;
export const euler = 2.7182;
```

Now we can use these values in other files, using the `type="module"` in HTML files, as in Listing 5-3, or `import` in JS files, as in Listing 5-4.

Listing 5-3. Using ES Modules in HTML

```
<script type="module" src="./math-constants.js"></script>
```

Listing 5-4. Using ES Modules in JS Scripts

```
import {pi, euler} from "./math-constants.js";
```

Figure 5-1 offers a graphical view of ES Modules.

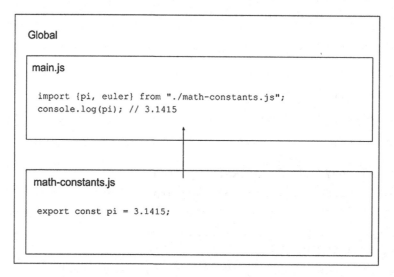

Figure 5-1. *Graphical representation of ES Modules*

Building the MathOperationsComponent

To practice with Shadow DOM, we are going to build a simple component called <math-operations-component> to add social networks links in our apps. This component receives two parameters, 'operation' and 'initialValue', in which 'getCircumference' receives the circumference with a radius; getCalcOneYear gets the compound interest for one year with two parameters, the interest rate and the current value; and 'getLog2' returns the natural logarithm value of 2.

First, we are going to define our component, as in Listing 5-5.

Listing 5-5. Defining MathOperationsComponent

```
class MathOperationsComponent extends HTMLElement {

    constructor() {
    }

}
customElements.define('math-operations-component',
MathOperationsComponent);
```

Create a new math-constants.js file in the same level as index.html and create the constants pi, euler, and ln2, employing the 'export' to allow using these values as a module, as in Listing 5-6.

Listing 5-6. Defining MathOperationsComponent

```
export const pi = 3.1415;
export const euler = 2.7182;
export const ln2 = 0.693;
```

Now, in the file index.html, we must add a couple of things, in order to use the module in the component, as in Listing 5-7.

Listing 5-7. Using Modules in MathOperationsComponent

```
<script type="module">
import {pi, euler, ln2} from './math-constants.js';

class MathOperationsComponent extends HTMLElement {

    constructor() {
    }

}
customElements.define('math-operations-component',
MathOperationsComponent);
</script>
```

First in the preceding code snippet is type="module" in the script tag for modules in our code. Second is 'import', for constants that we declared in math-constants.js.

Now, in our component, we are going to create getCircumference, getCalcOneYear, and getLN2, to return the value that we require for the parameters that we sent in the call. This is shown in Listing 5-8.

Listing 5-8. Using Modules in MathOperationsComponent

```
    getCircumference(radius) {
        return 2 * pi * radius;
    }

    getCalcOneYear(interestRate, currentVal) {
        return currentVal * (euler ** interestRate);
    }

    getLN2() {
        return ln2;
    }
```

Note that here we are using the constants that we imported from the module.

Finally, we add the logic in constructor(), to process the parameters that we send in the 'operation', and 'initialValue' attributes in the component, and create the methods for the template and styles that we want to reveal our information in the document, as in Listing 5-9.

Listing 5-9. Using Modules in MathOperationsComponent

```
<script type="module">
import {pi, euler, ln2} from './math-constants.js';

class MathOperationsComponent extends HTMLElement {

    constructor() {
        super();
        this.root = this.attachShadow({mode: 'open'});
        this.container = document.createElement('div');
        this.root.appendChild(this.container);

        switch(this.getAttribute('operation')) {
            case 'getCircumference':
                const radius = this.getAttribute('initialValue');
                this.container.innerHTML = MathOperationsComponent.
                getTemplate(this.getCircumference(radius));
                break;
            case 'getCalcOneYear':
                const [interestRate, currentVal] = this.getAttribute
                ('initialValue').split(',');
                this.container.innerHTML = MathOperationsComponent.get
                Template(this.getCalcOneYear(interestRate, currentVal));
                break;
            case 'getLog2':
                this.container.innerHTML = MathOperationsComponent.
                getTemplate(this.getLN2());
            break;
        }
    }

    getCircumference(radius) {
        return 2 * pi * radius;
    }
```

```
getCalcOneYear(interestRate, currentVal) {
    return currentVal * (euler ** interestRate);
}

getLN2() {
    return ln2;
}

static getTemplate(value) {
    return `
    ${MathOperationsComponent.getStyle()}
    <div>
        ${value}
    </div>
    `;
}

static getStyle() {
    return `
    <style>
        div {
            padding: 5px;
            background-color: yellow;
            color; black;
        }
    </style>`;
}
}
customElements.define('math-operations-component',
MathOperationsComponent);
</script>
```

To run our code, we must use a static server, because of security policies with the browsers and the modules. We can initialize a node application running from the root of our project

```
$npm init
```

and answering the questions in the terminal.

Later, in the package.json file, I added two things, shown in Listing 5-10.

Listing 5-10. Adding dependencies and npm Script in Package.json

```
...
"scripts": {
    "start": "serve",
    ...
  },
"devDependencies": {
    "serve": "^11.3.2"
  }
...
```

This instruction will install the 'serve' package in our project and, with 'npm run start', run a local server.

Then, to run our example, you must go inside our math-operations-component folder and run

```
$npm install
```

Later, run

```
$npm run start
```

Now go to http://localhost:5000, and that's it. You can see that our component is running (Figure 5-2).

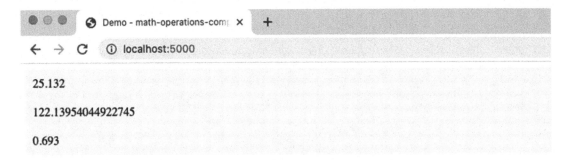

Figure 5-2. *Using ES Modules in Google Chrome with a local server*

You can access the source code for this book (`https://github.com/carlosrojaso/apress-book-web-components`) at `$git checkout chap-5`.

Summary

In this chapter, you learned the following:

- What ES Modules are and how to use them in web components

- How to create an ES Module

- How to use ES Modules to create a web component to add math functions in our web apps

CHAPTER 6

Component Architecture

In this chapter, you will learn how to design components and make them work together in a web application. We are going to connect our web application to an application programming interface (API) and define a dataflow for our components.

Our NoteApp Application

We will create a simple notes app that allows users to make notes, as illustrated in Figure 6-1. A new note will be created when users click a button, using a modal and a form with "Title" and "Description," after the user adds information. We must add this information to a Notes list that shows us all the notes the user has created in the past and removes notes from that list.

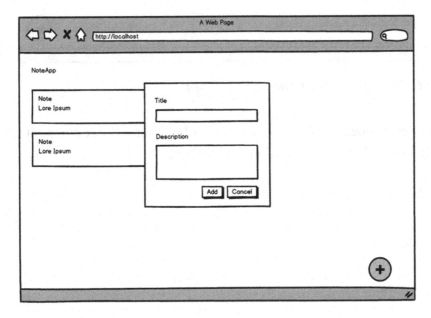

Figure 6-1. *NoteApp mock-up*

61

© Carlos Rojas 2021
C. Rojas, *Building Native Web Components*, https://doi.org/10.1007/978-1-4842-5905-4_6

Now we can take this initial mock-up and think about how we can split the elements into small pieces that will make our development easier and better oriented to components that we can use in the future.

In Figure 6-2, you can see that we have three main components (`simple-form-modal-component`, `note-list-component`, and `note-list-item-component`) that we can use inside the logic of `app.js` to achieve our goal of having a list of notes, the ability to remove notes, and allowance of the addition of new notes.

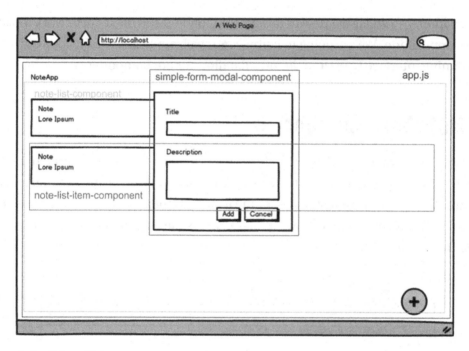

Figure 6-2. *Identifying components in our app*

With our components defined, we can think of a hierarchy of components (as in Figure 6-3), to see what the relationship among them is.

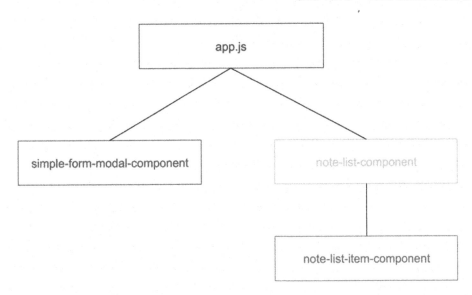

Figure 6-3. *Identifying the hierarchy of components in our app*

We can see that the main element is app.js. To it, we are going to add two sibling components, simple-form-modal-component and note-list-component, and inside of note-list-component, we will have several note-list-item-component elements that are children of note-list-component. Having a clear understanding of this relationship will help us with the other architectural decisions that we will be required to take in the next steps.

Communicating Between Web Components

When we are working with components, usually we need a way to send and receive data between parents and children (as in Figure 6-4), to update or send notification changes that a user or other component made at some moment in the business logic of our app. To achieve this, we use the properties to get data and events to send data to the other components.

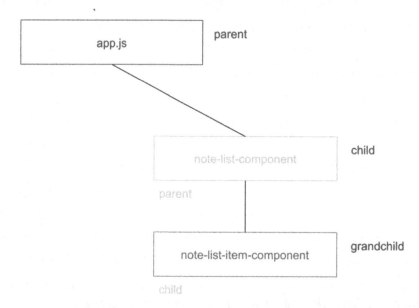

Figure 6-4. *Identifying communication between components*

In Figure 6-5, you can see that we are going to define passing data from the note-list-component using the idx and note attributes and receive data using the delEvent event.

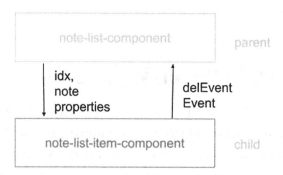

Figure 6-5. *Designing a communication mechanism between note-list-component and note-list-item-component*

This means that in our NoteListComponent, we are going to create the <note-list-item-component> elements that we require and pass an object note and a number idx, as you can see in Listing 6-1.

Listing 6-1. Defining `NoteListComponent`

```
class NoteListComponent extends HTMLElement {

    constructor() {
    }

    render() {
      return `
        <note-list-item-component note='${JSON.stringify(note)}'
        idx='${idx}'></note-list-item-component>`;
    }
}
customElements.define('note-list-component', NoteListComponent);
```

We are going to use `JSON.stringify()` to pass the object note correctly and `JSON.parse()` to receive that data in our child component. You can learn more about these methods at https://developer.mozilla.org/en-US/docs/Web/JavaScript/Reference/Global_Objects/JSON/stringify and https://developer.mozilla.org/en-US/docs/Web/JavaScript/Reference/Global_Objects/JSON/parse.

Now, in our `NotelistItemComponent`, we are going to create a custom event that `NoteListComponent` can listen to and that knows when the user wants to remove a note from the list, as shown in Listing 6-2.

Listing 6-2. Adding a Custom Event in `NoteListItemComponent`

```
class NoteListItemComponent extends HTMLElement {

    constructor() {
    }

    handleDelete() {
    this.dispatchEvent(new CustomEvent('delEvent', {bubbles: true,
    detail:  {idx: this.idx}}));
    }
}
customElements.define('note-list-item-component', NoteListItemComponent);
```

Here, we are creating a `handleDelete()` method that is using `CustomEvent()` to create an event and sending the data that we need in `detail`. In that way, the parent is going to know what item needs to be removed from the list. You can learn more about `CustomEvent` in `https://developer.mozilla.org/en-US/docs/Web/API/CustomEvent/CustomEvent`.

Usually, with properties and events, we can handle the communication between components in most of the scenarios on a small and medium scale. Still, if your app is more sophisticated and has complex interactions between components, you will require an event bus, which you can find at `www.npmjs.com/package/js-event-bus`, or a pattern such as Redux, which you can find at `https://github.com/reduxjs/redux`.

NoteListComponent

In the preceding section, you learned how to make our web components communicate. Now we are going to build these components. First, the more natural way to handle our notes is to receive an array of notes and create one item for each element. Then, we are going to get the attribute `notes` and use the method `JSON.parse()` to convert this into an object. We are using `_notes`, to avoid conflicts with the setter in the component and render all the notes again, each time that they are updated (see Listing 6-3).

Listing 6-3. `getter` and `setter` in `NoteListComponent`

```
class NoteListComponent extends HTMLElement {

    constructor() {
        super();

        this._notes = JSON.parse(this.getAttribute('notes')) || [];
        this.root = this.attachShadow({mode: 'open'});
        this.root.innerHTML = this.render();
    }

    render() {
        let noteElements = '';
        this._notes.map(
        (note, idx) => {
            noteElements += `
```

```
      <note-list-item-component note='${JSON.stringify(note)}'
      idx='${idx}'></note-list-item-component>`;
    }
  );
  return `
    ${noteElements}`;
  }

  get notes(){
    return this._notes;
  }

  set notes(newValue) {
    this._notes = newValue;
    this.root.innerHTML = this.render();
  }
}
customElements.define('note-list-component', NoteListComponent);
```

In addition, we are using a map() in the render method, to iterate in the object notes and create each item that we need, and updating the Shadow DOM with the list of items.

Remember that we are receiving a delEvent event each time that we need to remove an item from the list. Therefore, we must handle this behavior here, adding a listener for that event and eliminating the element from the list, as in Listing 6-4.

Listing 6-4. Adding a Listener in NoteListComponent

```
class NoteListComponent extends HTMLElement {

  constructor() {
    super();

    this._notes = JSON.parse(this.getAttribute('notes')) || [];
    this.root = this.attachShadow({mode: 'open'});
    this.root.innerHTML = this.render();
    this.handleDelEvent = this.handleDelEvent.bind(this);
  }
```

```
connectedCallback() {
  this.root.addEventListener('delEvent', this.handleDelEvent);
}

disconnectedCallback () {
  this.root.removeEventListener('delEvent', this.handleDelEvent);
}

handleDelEvent(e) {
  this._notes.splice(e.detail.idx, 1);
  this.root.innerHTML = this.render();
}

render() {
  let noteElements = '';
  this._notes.map(
  (note, idx) => {
    noteElements += `
    <note-list-item-component note='${JSON.stringify(note)}'
    idx='${idx}'></note-list-item-component>`;
  }
  );
  return `
  ${noteElements}`;
}

get notes(){
  return this._notes;
}

set notes(newValue) {
  this._notes = newValue;
  this.root.innerHTML = this.render();
}
}
customElements.define('note-list-component', NoteListComponent);
```

Here, we are adding the listener in connectedCallback() and removing the listener in disconnectedCallback(), to avoid unnecessary listeners when the component is removed. Also, we use bind() in the constructor, to indicate in the constructor that we are defining the handleDelEvent() and ensure that it doesn't get undefined when we want to pass the method in our component. With these modifications, our component is complete.

NoteListItemComponent

Now the NoteListComponent creates a list of <note-list-item-component> elements and passes a note object and an idx number that is equivalent to the position in the array of notes. We are going to add the getters and setters in NoteListItemComponent and initialize these properties in the constructor(). Remember that a note is an object, and with JSON.parse(), we are going to convert this data into an object (see Listing 6-5).

Listing 6-5. Adding Getters and Setters in NoteListItemComponent

```
class NoteListItemComponent extends HTMLElement {

  constructor() {
    super();

    this._note = JSON.parse(this.getAttribute('note')) || {};
    this.idx = this.getAttribute('idx') || -1;
    this.root = this.attachShadow({mode: 'open'});
  }

  get note() {
    return this._note;
  }

  set note(newValue) {
    this._note = newValue;
  }

  get idx() {
    return this._idx;
  }
```

```
set idx(newValue) {
  this._idx = newValue;
}

handleDelete() {
  this.dispatchEvent(new CustomEvent('delEvent', {bubbles: true, detail:
  {idx: this.idx}}));
}
customElements.define('note-list-item-component', NoteListItemComponent);
```

We are going to add the template of this component and the styles, to get a nice item for the notes (see Listing 6-6).

Listing 6-6. Adding the Template and Styles in NoteListItemComponent

```
class NoteListItemComponent extends HTMLElement {

  constructor() {
    super();

    this._note = JSON.parse(this.getAttribute('note')) || {};
    this.idx = this.getAttribute('idx') || -1;
    this.root = this.attachShadow({mode: 'open'});
    this.root.innerHTML = this.getTemplate();
  }

  get note() {
    return this._note;
  }

  set note(newValue) {
    this._note = newValue;
  }

  get idx() {
    return this._idx;
  }
```

```
  set idx(newValue) {
    this._idx = newValue;
  }

  handleDelete() {
    this.dispatchEvent(new CustomEvent('delEvent', {bubbles: true, detail:
    {idx: this.idx}}));
  }
  getStyle() {
    return `
    <style>
      .note {
        background-color: #ffffcc;
        border-left: 6px solid #ffeb3b;
      }
      div {
        margin: 5px 0px 5px;
        padding: 4px 12px;
      }
    </style>
    `;
  }

  getTemplate() {
    return`
    ${this.getStyle()}
    <div class="note">
      <p><strong>${this._note.title}</strong> ${this._note.description}</p>
      <br/>
      <button type="button" id="deleteButton">Delete</button>
    </div>`;
  }
}
customElements.define('note-list-item-component', NoteListItemComponent);
```

With these enhancements, our <note-list-item-component> is going to look like Figure 6-6.

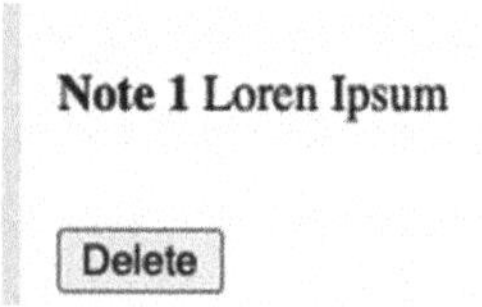

Note 1 Loren Ipsum

Delete

Figure 6-6. *note-list-item component in Google Chrome*

Finally, we are going to add an event listener for the Delete button that triggers the delEvent event. As with NoteListComponent, we must add the listener in connectedCallback() and remove it in disconnectedCallback(), as shown in Listing 6-7.

Listing 6-7. Adding an Event Listener in NoteListItemComponent

```
class NoteListItemComponent extends HTMLElement {

  constructor() {
    super();

    this._note = JSON.parse(this.getAttribute('note')) || {};
    this.idx = this.getAttribute('idx') || -1;
    this.root = this.attachShadow({mode: 'open'});
    this.root.innerHTML = this.getTemplate();
    this.handleDelete = this.handleDelete.bind(this);
  }

  connectedCallback() {
    this.delBtn.addEventListener('click', this.handleDelete);
  }

  disconnectedCallback () {
    this.delBtn.removeEventListener('click', this.handleDelete);
  }

  get note() {
    return this._note;
  }

  set note(newValue) {
    this._note = newValue;
  }
```

```
get idx() {
  return this._idx;
}

set idx(newValue) {
  this._idx = newValue;
}

handleDelete() {
  this.dispatchEvent(new CustomEvent('delEvent', {bubbles: true,
  detail: {idx: this.idx}}));
}

getStyle() {
  return `
  <style>
    .note {
      background-color: #ffffcc;
      border-left: 6px solid #ffeb3b;
    }
    div {
      margin: 5px 0px 5px;
      padding: 4px 12px;
    }
  </style>
  `;
}

getTemplate() {
  return`
  ${this.getStyle()}
  <div class="note">
    <p><strong>${this._note.title}</strong> ${this._note.description}
    </p><br/>
    <button type="button" id="deleteButton">Delete</button>
  </div>`;
}
}
customElements.define('note-list-item-component', NoteListItemComponent);
```

Now the NoteListItemComponent is going to send the custom event when a user clicks on the Delete button, and NoteListComponent will know what the item that must be eliminated from the list is.

SimpleFormModalComponent

With NoteListComponent and NoteListItemComponent ready, we now require an easy way to add new notes in our app. That is why we are going to create the SimpleFormModalComponent, a form that is going to allow users to input a title and description. This component is going to communicate with app.js, with which we are going to use an open property, to know when to show or hide the modal and when the user inserts data in the form. We are going to pass that data with the custom event addEvent, as shown in Figure 6-7.

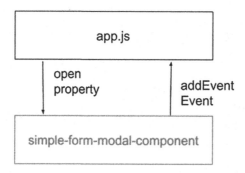

Figure 6-7. *Identifying communication between* simple-form-modal-component *and* app.js

We are going to start defining our component, adding setters and getters, as in Listing 6-8.

Listing 6-8. Adding Getters and Setters in SimpleFormModalComponent

```
class SimpleFormModalComponent extends HTMLElement {

  constructor() {
    super();

    this.root = this.attachShadow({mode: 'open'});
    this.container = document.createElement('div');
```

```
    this.container.innerHTML = this.getTemplate();
    this.root.appendChild(this.container.cloneNode(true));

    this._open = this.getAttribute('open') || false;
  }
  get open() {
    return this._open;
  }

  set open(newValue) {
    this._open = newValue;
  }
}
customElements.define('simple-form-modal-component',
SimpleFormModalComponent);
```

Now we are going to add the template and styles required to show and hide the component (see Listing 6-9).

Listing 6-9. Adding the Template and Styles in `SimpleFormModalComponent`

```
class SimpleFormModalComponent extends HTMLElement {

  constructor() {
      super();
      this.root = this.attachShadow({mode: 'open'});
      this.container = document.createElement('div');
      this.container.innerHTML = this.getTemplate();
      this.root.appendChild(this.container.cloneNode(true));

      this._open = this.getAttribute('open') || false;
  }
  get open() {
    return this._open;
  }
  set open(newValue) {
    this._open = newValue;
  }
  getTemplate() {
```

```
    return `
    ${this.getStyle()}
    <div id="myModal" class="modal">
      <div class="modal-content">
        <form id="myForm">
          <label for="ftitle">Title:</label><br>
          <input type="text" id="ftitle" name="ftitle"><br>
          <label for="fdesc">Description:</label><br>
          <textarea id="fdesc" name="fdesc" rows="4" cols="50">
          </textarea><br/>
          <button type="button" id="addBtn">Add</button><button type=
          "button" id="closeBtn">Close</button>
        </form>
      </div>
    </div>`;
  }

  getStyle() {
    return `
    <style>
      .modal {
        display: none;
        position: fixed;
        z-index: 1;
        padding-top: 100px;
        left: 0;
        top: 0;
        width: 100%;
        height: 100%;
        overflow: auto;
        background-color: rgb(0,0,0);
        background-color: rgba(0,0,0,0.4);
      }
      .modal-content {
        background-color: #fefefe;
        margin: auto;
```

```
      padding: 20px;
      border: 1px solid #888;
      width: 50%;
    }
    .close {
      color: #aaaaaa;
      float: right;
      font-size: 28px;
      font-weight: bold;
    }

    .close:hover,
    .close:focus {
      color: #000;
      text-decoration: none;
      cursor: pointer;
    }
  </style>`;
  }
}
customElements.define('simple-form-modal-component',
SimpleFormModalComponent);
```

With this enhancement, we are going to show a form with two inputs and two buttons. The modal class will place the element on top of everything and show it in the middle of the window with a transparent gray background. Also, because the default display is "none", that means that we are going to hide this element and make it visible when we set that property to "block". To handle this behavior, we are going to create the method showModal() and trigger it in the setter of the open property, as in Listing 6-10.

Listing 6-10. Adding showModal() in SimpleFormModalComponent

```
class SimpleFormModalComponent extends HTMLElement {
  constructor() {
    super();

    this.root = this.attachShadow({mode: 'open'});
    this.container = document.createElement('div');
```

```
      this.container.innerHTML = this.getTemplate();
      this.root.appendChild(this.container.cloneNode(true));

      this._open = this.getAttribute('open') || false;
      this.modal = this.root.getElementById("myModal");
  }
  get open() {
    return this._open;
  }
  set open(newValue) {
    this._open = newValue;
    this.showModal(this._open);
  }
  showModal(state) {
    if(state) {
      this.modal.style.display = "block";
    } else {
      this.modal.style.display = "none"
    }
  }
  getTemplate() {
      return `
      ${this.getStyle()}
      <div id="myModal" class="modal">
        <div class="modal-content">
          <form id="myForm">
            <label for="ftitle">Title:</label><br>
            <input type="text" id="ftitle" name="ftitle"><br>
            <label for="fdesc">Description:</label><br>
            <textarea id="fdesc" name="fdesc" rows="4" cols="50">
            </textarea><br/>
            <button type="button" id="addBtn">Add</button><button
            type="button" id="closeBtn">Close</button>
          </form>
        </div>
      </div>`;
  }
```

```
getStyle() {
    return `
    <style>
      .modal {
        display: none;
        position: fixed;
        z-index: 1;
        padding-top: 100px;
        left: 0;
        top: 0;
        width: 100%;
        height: 100%;
        overflow: auto;
        background-color: rgb(0,0,0);
        background-color: rgba(0,0,0,0.4);
      }
      .modal-content {
        background-color: #fefefe;
        margin: auto;
        padding: 20px;
        border: 1px solid #888;
        width: 50%;
      }
      .close {
        color: #aaaaaa;
        float: right;
        font-size: 28px;
        font-weight: bold;
      }

      .close:hover,
      .close:focus {
        color: #000;
```

```
          text-decoration: none;
          cursor: pointer;
        }
      </style>`;
  }
}
customElements.define('simple-form-modal-component',
SimpleFormModalComponent);
```

And, finally, we are going to create the events for the button and send a custom event when the user adds a note (see Listing 6-11).

Listing 6-11. Adding Events in SimpleFormModalComponent

```
class SimpleFormModalComponent extends HTMLElement {

  constructor() {
      super();

      this.root = this.attachShadow({mode: 'open'});
      this.container = document.createElement('div');
      this.container.innerHTML = this.getTemplate();
      this.root.appendChild(this.container.cloneNode(true));

      this._open = this.getAttribute('open') || false;

      this.modal = this.root.getElementById("myModal");
      this.addBtn = this.root.getElementById("addBtn");
      this.closeBtn = this.root.getElementById("closeBtn");

      this.handleAdd = this.handleAdd.bind(this);
      this.handleCancel = this.handleCancel.bind(this);

  }

  connectedCallback() {
    this.addBtn.addEventListener('click', this.handleAdd);
    this.closeBtn.addEventListener('click', this.handleCancel);
  }
```

```
disconnectedCallback () {
  this.addBtn.removeEventListener('click', this.handleAdd);
  this.closeBtn.removeEventListener('click', this.handleCancel);
}

get open() {
  return this._open;
}

set open(newValue) {
  this._open = newValue;
  this.showModal(this._open);
}

handleAdd() {
  const fTitle = this.root.getElementById('ftitle');
  const fDesc = this.root.getElementById('fdesc');
  this.dispatchEvent(new CustomEvent('addEvent', {detail: {title: fTitle.
  value, description: fDesc.value}}));

  fTitle.value = '';
  fDesc.value = '';
  this.open = false;
}

handleCancel() {
  this.open = false;
}

showModal(state) {
  if(state) {
    this.modal.style.display = "block";
  } else {
    this.modal.style.display = "none"
  }
}
```

```
getTemplate() {
    return `
    ${this.getStyle()}
    <div id="myModal" class="modal">
      <div class="modal-content">
        <form id="myForm">
          <label for="ftitle">Title:</label><br>
          <input type="text" id="ftitle" name="ftitle"><br>
          <label for="fdesc">Description:</label><br>
          <textarea id="fdesc" name="fdesc" rows="4" cols="50">
          </textarea><br/>
          <button type="button" id="addBtn">Add</button><button
          type="button" id="closeBtn">Close</button>
        </form>
      </div>
    </div>`;
}

getStyle() {
    return `
    <style>
      .modal {
        display: none;
        position: fixed;
        z-index: 1;
        padding-top: 100px;
        left: 0;
        top: 0;
        width: 100%;
        height: 100%;
        overflow: auto;
        background-color: rgb(0,0,0);
        background-color: rgba(0,0,0,0.4);
      }
```

```
      .modal-content {
        background-color: #fefefe;
        margin: auto;
        padding: 20px;
        border: 1px solid #888;
        width: 50%;
      }
      .close {
        color: #aaaaaa;
        float: right;
        font-size: 28px;
        font-weight: bold;
      }

      .close:hover,
      .close:focus {
        color: #000;
        text-decoration: none;
        cursor: pointer;
      }
    </style>`;
  }
}
customElements.define('simple-form-modal-component',
SimpleFormModalComponent);
```

This code is similar to that we made for NoteListComponent and NoteListItemComponent. We are adding the listener in connectedCallback(), removing it in disconnectedCallback(), and sending the custom event in handleAdd(). Now we have a modal (see Figure 6-8).

Figure 6-8. `simple-form-modal-component` in Google Chrome

Adding an API

Usually, when you are working on a web app, you must connect your app to services. We will use API Rest to connect the open API `https://jsonplaceholder.typicode.com/`. This API has all the HTTP methods (GET, POST, PUT, PATCH, DELETE) that you can use in a real-life app.

Call API methods are common in all parts of our app. Therefore, we probably are going to reuse these methods in several components. This is why we are going to build a small module with calls and, in future, only import it and use the function that we require (see Listing 6-12).

Listing 6-12. Creating `notes-data-api.js`

```
const apiUrl= 'https://jsonplaceholder.typicode.com';
export const notesDataApi = {
    createTask(task) {
        return fetch(`${apiUrl}/posts/`, {
            method: 'POST',
            body: JSON.stringify(task),
            headers: {
              "Content-type": "application/json; charset=UTF-8"
            }
        });
```

```
    },
  deleteTask(id) {
      return fetch(`${apiUrl}/posts/${id}`, {method: 'DELETE'});
    },
  getTasks(id) {
      return fetch(`${apiUrl}/users/${id}/posts`);
    }
};
```

In this module, we are creating functions to create, get, and delete a task. These functions are going to use Mozilla (`https://developer.mozilla.org/en-US/docs/Web/API/Fetch_API`) to make the HTTP request to the API and return the data that we require.

Now that we have all the small pieces that we require for our app, we are going to put everything together. First, we are going to create an `index.html` and call all the components and modules that we are using, as in Listing 6-13.

Listing 6-13. Creating `index.html`

```
<!DOCTYPE html>
<html>
<head>
  <meta name="viewport" content="width=device-width, initial-scale=1">
  <script async src="./simple-form-modal-component/simple-form-modal-
  component.js"></script>
  <script async type="module" src="./note-list-component/note-list-
  component.js"></script>
  <script async src="./note-list-item-component/note-list-item-
  component.js"></script>
  <link rel="stylesheet" type="text/css" href="./style.css">
</head>
<body>

  <h2>Notes App</h2>
  <button class="fab" id="myBtn">+</button>
  <simple-form-modal-component></simple-form-modal-component>
  <note-list-component></note-list-component>
</body>
</html>
```

In the index.html, we are adding a button that is going to show the modal when the user must add a new note, and we are going to create app.js a small logic for the index. html that is going to connect all the pieces (see Listing 6-14).

Listing 6-14. Creating app.js

```
import { notesDataApi } from './utils/notes-data-api.js';
const formModal = document.querySelector('simple-form-modal-component');
const noteList = document.querySelector('note-list-component');

notesDataApi.getTasks(1)
  .then((res) => res.json())
  .then((items) => {
    const allNotes = items.map((item)=>({title: item.title, description:
    item.body}));
    noteList.notes = allNotes;
  });

formModal.addEventListener('addEvent', function(e) {
  let notes = noteList.notes;

  notes.push({"title": e.detail.title, "description": e.detail.
  description});
  noteList.notes = notes;
});

const myBtn = document.getElementById('myBtn');
myBtn.addEventListener('click', function() {
  formModal.open = !formModal.open;
});
```

Here, we are adding the login for the button that we add in the index.html. This button is going to pass a state to the SimpleFormModalComponent, to show or hide the modal. We are adding a listener for the custom event addEvent, to get the data for the new note and pass this data to the NoteListComponent. We are using the note-data-api module to get all the notes that we have in the API and send this data to the NoteListComponent, to fill dummy notes by default. Finally, we are going to add a style file, to improve the appearance of our button in index.html, as in Listing 6-15.

Listing 6-15. Creating `style.css`

```
.fab {
  width: 50px;
  height: 50px;
  background-color: black;
  border-radius: 50%;
  border: 1px solid black;
  transition: all 0.1s ease-in-out;

  font-size: 30px;
  color: white;
  text-align: center;
  line-height: 50px;

  position: fixed;
  right: 20px;
  bottom: 20px;
}

.fab:hover {
  box-shadow: 0 6px 14px 0 #666;
  transform: scale(1.05);
}
```

Now our NoteApp is complete and looks like Figure 6-9.

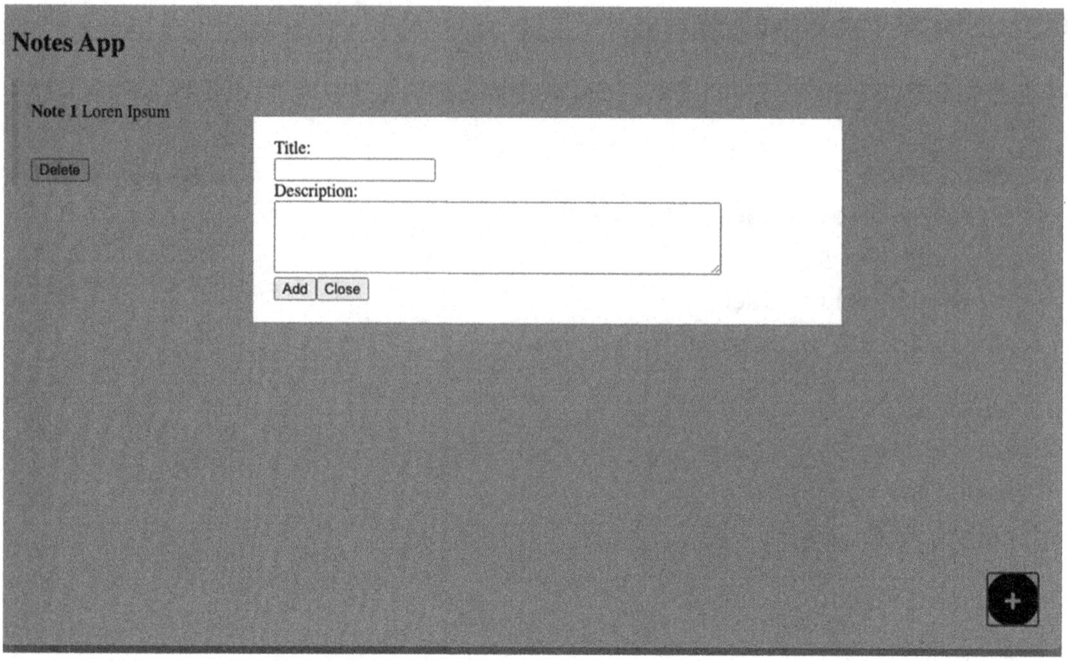

Figure 6-9. *NoteApp in Google Chrome*

You can access the source code for this book (`https://github.com/carlosrojaso/apress-book-web-components`) at `$git checkout chap-6`.

Summary

In this chapter, you learned

- How to design components in a real web app

- How to make all the components work together with properties and custom events

- How to connect our app to an API

CHAPTER 7

Distributing Web Components

In this chapter, you will learn how to make our web components available in npm. You are also going to learn about the browser support offered by Web Components APIS, how to add polyfills to support more web browsers, and how to add Webpack and Babel to process and prepare our web components for publication.

Publishing to npm

In Chapter 6, we created three components: `<simple-form-modal-component>`, `<note-list-component>`, and `<note-list-item-component>`. Now we are going to make these components available through `www.npmjs.com`.npm is a repository of packages that we can add in our projects easily with the command $npm install `<package>`.

First, we require an account to publish packages (see Figure 7-1).

© Carlos Rojas 2021
C. Rojas, *Building Native Web Components*, https://doi.org/10.1007/978-1-4842-5905-4_7

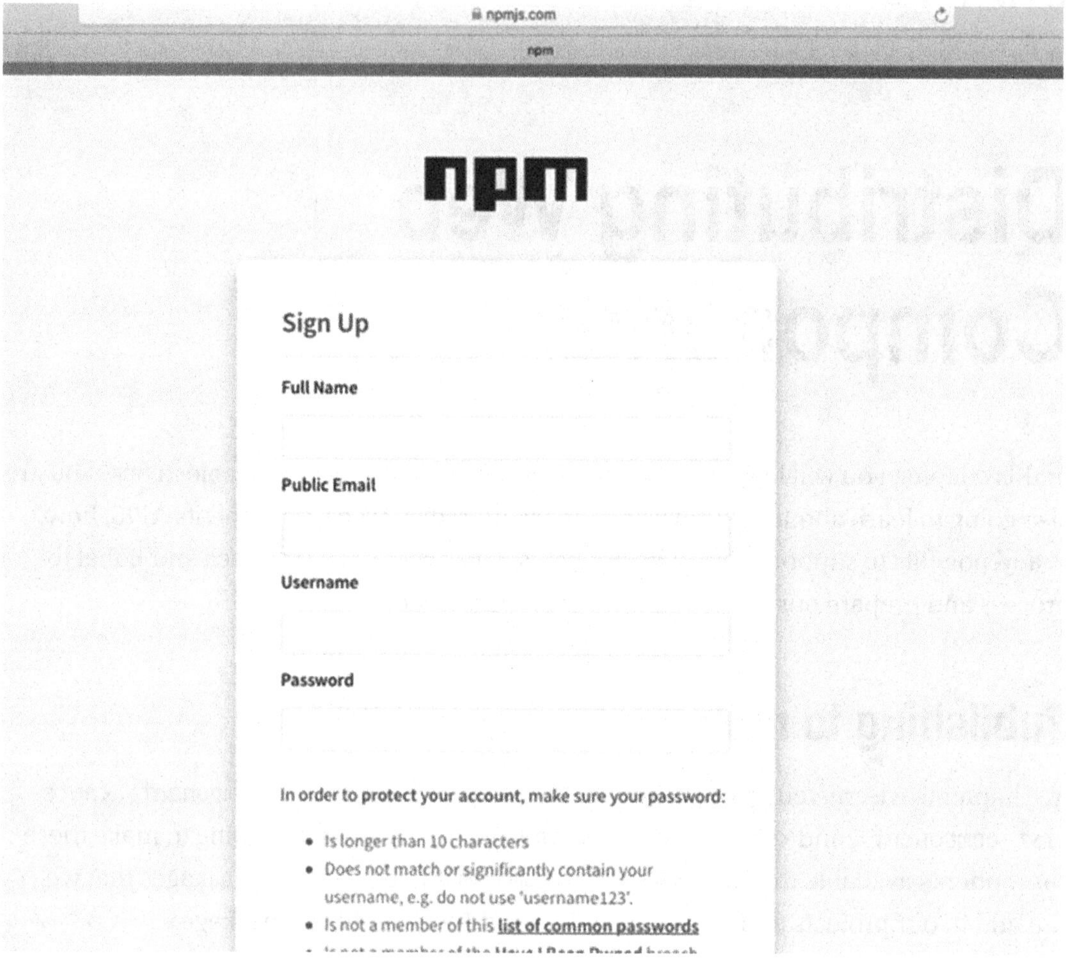

Figure 7-1. *Creating a user account in npmjs.com*

Next, we must connect our account with our terminal, using $npm adduser (Figure 7-2).

```
carlosrojaso@Carloss-MacBook-Pro apress-book-web-components % npm adduser
Username: carlosrojaso
Password:
Email: (this IS public) ing.carlosandresrojas@pm.me
Logged in as carlosrojaso on https://registry.npmjs.org/.
carlosrojaso@Carloss-MacBook-Pro apress-book-web-components % █
```

Figure 7-2. *Connecting our terminal with npm*

Now we must separate our components and make them modules, with the structure shown in Figure 7-3.

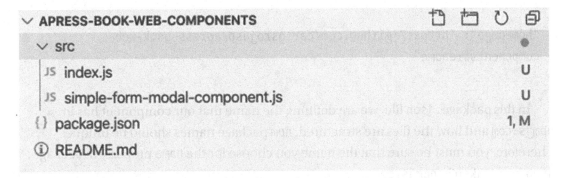

Figure 7-3. *Structure to publish components*

We create a package.json file for the component, as in Listing 7-1.

Listing 7-1. package.json for simple-form-modal-component

```json
{
  "name": "apress-simple-form-modal-component",
  "version": "1.0.1",
  "description": "simple form modal component",
  "main": "src/index.js",
  "module": "src/index.js",
  "directories": {
    "src": "src"
  },
  "scripts": {
    "test": "echo \"Error: no test specified\" && exit 1"
  },
  "repository": {
    "type": "git",
    "url": "git+https://github.com/carlosrojaso/apress-book-web-components.
    git"
  },
  "author": "Carlos Rojas",
  "license": "MIT",
```

```
"bugs": {
  "url": "https://github.com/carlosrojaso/apress-book-web-components/
  issues"
},
"homepage": "https://github.com/carlosrojaso/apress-book-web-
components#readme"
}
```

In this package.json file, we are defining the name that our component has in npmjs.com and how the files are structured. npm package names should be unique. Therefore, you must be sure that the name you choose for the name property in package.json is not taken in npmjs.com.

Now we are going to create a directory called src, in which we are going to locate our code source. Then, we are going to move our simple-form-modal-component.js there and create a new file index.js, as in Listing 7-2.

Listing 7-2. index.js for simple-form-modal-component

```
export * from './simple-form-modal-component';
```

This is just one line with which we are importing everything in simple-form-modal-componet.js. Therefore, in our file simple-form-modal-component.js, we must add the word *export*, to make our component available as a module, as in Listing 7-3.

Listing 7-3. Converting simple-form-modal-component in a Module

```
export class SimpleFormModalComponent extends HTMLElement {
...
}
customElements.define('simple-form-modal-component', SimpleFormModal
Component);
```

OK, we have our component ready for now. The next step is run

```
$npm publish
```

Now we have published our component (see Figure 7-4).

```
carlosrojaso@Carloss-MacBook-Pro apress-book-web-components % npm publish

              📦   apress-simple-form-modal-component@1.0.0
         === Tarball Contents ===
         994B   package.json
         920B   README.md
         46B    simple-form-modal-component/index.js
         3.1kB  simple-form-modal-component/simple-form-modal-component.js
         === Tarball Details ===
         name:            apress-simple-form-modal-component
         version:         1.0.0
         package size:    2.0 kB
         unpacked size:   5.1 kB
         shasum:          cdf272f46a1009448398acabbfb335516474cb10
         integrity:       sha512-GTZ/lREcpWpzj[...]YNzjYNshL2HqQ==
         total files:     4

+ apress-simple-form-modal-component@1.0.0
```

Figure 7-4. *Publishing* `simple-form-modal-component`

You can access the code for this book (https://github.com/carlosrojaso/apress-book-web-components) at $git checkout chap-7-1.

This process is similar for <note-list-component> and <note-list-item-component>. If you want to see the modifications, you can do so at $git checkout chap-7-2 and $git checkout chap-7-3.

Now we can easily use our components in our projects. For now, we are going to use the service unpkg.com. unpkg is cdn for npm packages, to insert our packages easily, as shown in Listing 7-4.

Listing 7-4. `package.json` for `simple-form-modal-component`

```
<!DOCTYPE html>
<html>
<head>

<meta name="viewport" content="width=device-width, initial-scale=1">

<script async type="module" src="http://unpkg.com/apress-simple-form-modal-
component@1.0.1/src/simple-form-modal-component.js"></script>
```

```
<script async type="module" src="http://unpkg.com/apress-book-web-
components-note-list@1.0.1/src/note-list-component.js"></script>
<script async type="module" src="http://unpkg.com/apress-note-list-item-
component@1.0.1/src/note-list-item-component.js"></script>

<script async type="module" src="./app.js"></script>

<link rel="stylesheet" type="text/css" href="./style.css">

</head>
<body>
<h2>Notes App</h2>

<button class="fab" id="myBtn">+</button>

<simple-form-modal-component></simple-form-modal-component>

<note-list-component></note-list-component>

</body>
</html>
```

You can access the code (https://github.com/carlosrojaso/apress-book-web-components) at $git checkout chap-7-4.

With these modifications, we don't require our components files in our project, because we are importing from unpkg.com. In the next sections, you are going to learn to add other tools to run everything from our local environment, using npm without unpkg.com.

Old Web Browsers Support

Web Components have excellent support in major browsers or Webkit and all Chrome-based web browsers (see Figure 7-5). But what happens if we must support a web browser such as IE 11?

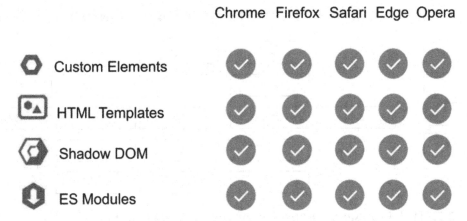

Figure 7-5. *Major browsers supporting Web Components' main specifications*

If you go to Can I use (`caniuse.com`) and do a search for each specification that we require to work with Web Components, you will find that for ES6, IE 11 has limited support (Figure 7-6).

	IE	Chrome	Firefox	Safari	Edge
		4-20	2-5	3.1-7	12-14
Supported		21-50	6-53	7.1-9.1	15-18
Partial	6-10	51-81	54-79	10-13	79-83
Not Supported	11	83	80	13.1	84
		84-86	81-82	14-TP	

Figure 7-6. *Web browser versions supporting ES6[1]*

IE 11 doesn't offer support for custom elements (Figure 7-7).

---

[1]https://caniuse.com/es6

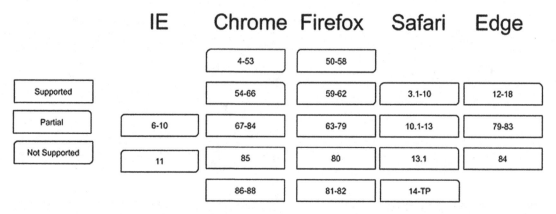

Figure 7-7. *Web browser versions supporting custom elements*[2]

IE 11 doesn't offer support for HTML templates (Figure 7-8).

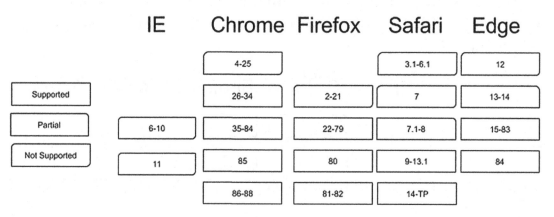

Figure 7-8. *Web browser versions supporting HTML templates*[3]

IE 11 doesn't offer support for Shadow DOM (Figure 7-9).

[2]https://caniuse.com/custom-elementsv1
[3]https://caniuse.com/template

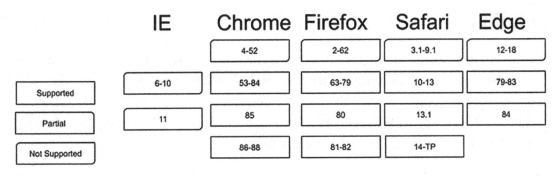

Figure 7-9. *Web browser versions supporting Shadow DOM[4]*

IE 11 doesn't offer support for ES modules (Figure 7-10).

	IE	Chrome	Firefox	Safari	Edge
		4-59	2-53	3.1-10	12-15
Supported		60	54-59	10.1	16-18
Partial	6-10	61-84	60-79	11-13	79-83
Not Supported	11	85	80	13.1	84
		86-88	81-82	14-TP	

Figure 7-10. *Web Browser versions supporting ES modules[5]*

IE 11 is a web browser that isn't popular yet; therefore, we are probably going to face problems at some point with some project. Fortunately, we can solve these problems with polyfills.

---

[4]https://caniuse.com/shadowdomv1
[5]https://caniuse.com/es6-module

Polyfills

Polyfills are used to add missing features to web browsers, through libraries that simulate these capabilities. For web components, there is a reliable package that we can add to our projects to support more web browsers. You can access the project at https://github.com/webcomponents/polyfills/tree/master/packages/webcomponentsjs and add the polyfills quickly, using unpkg.com (Listing 7-5).

Listing 7-5. Adding webcomponentsjs Polyfills

```
<!DOCTYPE html>
<html>
<head>
<meta name="viewport" content="width=device-width, initial-scale=1">
<script async src="https://unpkg.com/browse/@webcomponents/
webcomponentsjs@2.4.3/webcomponents-bundle.js"></script>
<script async type="module" src="http://unpkg.com/apress-simple-form-modal-
component@1.0.1/src/simple-form-modal-component.js"></script>
<script async type="module" src="http://unpkg.com/apress-book-web-
components-note-list@1.0.1/src/note-list-component.js"></script>
<script async type="module" src="http://unpkg.com/apress-note-list-item-
component@1.0.1/src/note-list-item-component.js"></script>
<script async type="module" src="./app.js"></script>
<link rel="stylesheet" type="text/css" href="./style.css">
</head>
<body>

<h2>Notes App</h2>
<button class="fab" id="myBtn">+</button>
<simple-form-modal-component></simple-form-modal-component>
<note-list-component></note-list-component>
</body>
</html>
```

With this modification, we now have better support for web browsers lacking the Web Components APIs.

You can access the code for this book (https://github.com/carlosrojaso/apress-book-web-components) at $git checkout chap-7-5.

Webpack and Babel

With polyfills, we now have the features previously missing in our project. Still, we require that IE 11 understand the JS that we are using with ES6. To make this possible, we are going to use Babel as a transpiler and convert our code in ES5. Webpack will handle all the dependencies and put everything together in a place where web browsers without ES modules can find it. You can read more about these tools at babeljs.io and webpack.js.org.

First, in each component, we are going to install the tools that we need for all the processes that we require, through npm. To do this, run the following:

$ npm install rimraf webpack webpack-cli babel-core babel-loader babel-preset-env path serve copyfiles --save-dev

With this command, you are going to add all the tools to package.json. For this example, I'm working with the simple-form-modal-component.

Now I am going to create a webpack.config.js file and add some settings (Listing 7-6).

Listing 7-6. Adding webpack.config.js in simple-form-modal-component Project

```
var path= require('path');
module.exports = {
  entry: './src/index.js',
  output: {
    path: path.resolve(__dirname, 'dist'),
    filename: 'index.js',
    library: 'apressSimpleFormModalComponent',
    libraryTarget: 'umd'
  }
};
```

Here, we are saying take the file in ./src/index.js and resolve all the dependencies, put them in ./dist/index.js, and handle that as a library in umd format. Universal Module Definition, or UMD, is a way to create modules before JS modules were added in web browsers.

Now we will add some npm scripts in our project (Listing 7-7).

Listing 7-7. Adding npm Scripts in package.json

```
"scripts": {
    "clean": "rimraf dist",
    "build": "npm run clean && webpack --mode production",
    "cpdir": "copyfiles -V \"./dist/*.js\" \"./example\"",
    "start": "npm run build && npm run cpdir && serve example"
  }
```

clean removes any generated code from the previous build. cpdir copies the ./dist directory inside the ./example folder. build uses webpack to create the transpiled file and start to run a local server to see our compiled component running in a sample.

Now I am going to create a sample folder and copy in it our complete NoteApp project, as you can find in the branch chap-7-5. To test our build, we must modify the index.html, as in Listing 7-8.

Listing 7-8. Loading Our simple-form-modal-component from ./dist/index.js

```
<!DOCTYPE html>
<html>

<head>

<meta name="viewport" content="width=device-width, initial-scale=1">

<script async src="https://unpkg.com/browse/@webcomponents/
webcomponentsjs@2.4.3/webcomponents-bundle.js"></script>

<script async src="./dist/index.js"></script>

<script async type="module" src="http://unpkg.com/apress-book-web-
components-note-list@1.0.1/src/note-list-component.js"></script>
```

```
<script async type="module" src="http://unpkg.com/apress-note-list-item-
component@1.0.1/src/note-list-item-component.js"></script>

<script async type="module" src="./app.js"></script>

<link rel="stylesheet" type="text/css" href="./style.css">
</head>
```

...

With this, each time we run a new build, we can test whether the compiled file is still working as expected.

Now you can run the command $npm run start and go to localhost:5000, to see if everything is working as expected (Figure 7-11).

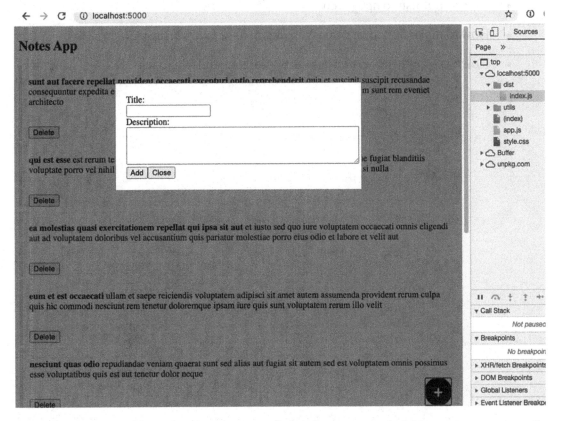

Figure 7-11. *Running simple-form-modal from a compiled file*

It's working as expected—and now we can use this in older web browsers, such as IE 11—and is using ES5, a JS specification that IE 11 should understand.

You can access the code (`https://github.com/carlosrojaso/apress-book-web-components`) with `$git checkout chap-7-6`.

This process is similar for `<note-list-component>` and `<note-list-item-component>`. If you want to see the modifications, you can access them from `$git checkout chap-7-7` and `$git checkout chap-7-8`.

And you can find the final example using polyfills and compiled components at `$git checkout chap-7`.

Summary

In this chapter, you learned

- How to publish to `npmjs.com`

- How to make our components available to old web browsers

- How to compile our components with Babel and Webpack

CHAPTER 8

Polymer

In this chapter, you will learn how to build web components with Polymer, why Polymer is used instead of VanillaJS, how to use `LitElement` in our web components, and how to use `lit-html`.

Polymer has been around a long time, starting with Polymer versions 1x and 2x. The project was focused on building a complete framework with which to make complete projects, using the Polymer CLI and `PolymerElements`. With Polymer 3x, you can still use the Polymer CLI and `PolymerElements`. However, the project is now oriented to use `LitElement` and `LitHtml` libraries to build components and make them available in all JS projects. That is why we are going to focus on these libraries.

Such large companies as Google, YouTube, Coca-Cola, McDonald's, and BBVA, among many others, build projects with Polymer.

Getting Started

To start building our components, Polymer provides two amazing "starters" that let us develop components with `LitElement` and give us some handy tools for linting, testing, and generating docs. You don't have to use the starter, but it will make things easier. You can get the JS Starter at `https://github.com/PolymerLabs/lit-element-starter-js` and the TS Starter at `https://github.com/PolymerLabs/lit-element-starter-ts`. I will use the JS Starter to build the examples in this chapter.

First, clone the project in your machine by running `$ git clone` (available at `https://github.com/PolymerLabs/lit-element-starter-js.git`).

Install dependencies, running in the project folder `$ npm install`.

And that's it. Now you can run a local server, by executing `$ npm run serve`.

Go to `http://localhost:8000/dev/` to see a sample web component running as in Figure 8-1.

C. Rojas, *Building Native Web Components*, https://doi.org/10.1007/978-1-4842-5905-4_8

Figure 8-1. *Hello, World! example*

You can run ESLint by executing $npm run lint.

The terminal will show all the code styling problems that are found in your component (see Figure 8-2).

```
> lit-element-starter-js@0.0.0 lint /Users/carlosrojaso/Projects/lit-element-st
rter-js
> lit-analyzer my-element.js && eslint '**/*.js'

Analyzing 1 files...

✓ Found 0 problems in 1 file
```

Figure 8-2. *Running ESLint*

You can run tests with Karma, Chai, and Mocha by executing $ npm run test.

The terminal will show all the tests that we write for the component (see Figure 8-3).

```
> karma start karma.conf.cjs

START:
26 07 2020 16:23:17.024:WARN [filelist]: Pattern "/Users/carlosrojaso/Projects/lit-element-starter-
js/__snapshots__/**/*.md" does not match any file.
26 07 2020 16:23:17.073:INFO [karma-server]: Karma v4.4.1 server started at http://0.0.0.0:9876/
26 07 2020 16:23:17.073:INFO [launcher]: Launching browsers ChromeHeadlessNoSandbox with concurrenc
y unlimited
26 07 2020 16:23:17.083:INFO [launcher]: Starting browser ChromeHeadless
26 07 2020 16:23:17.593:INFO [HeadlessChrome 84.0.4147 (Mac OS X 10.15.6)]: Connected on socket i2i
RPsCAH4c09H-vAAAA with id 22384050
  my-element
    ✓ is defined
    ✓ renders with default values
    ✓ renders with a set name
    ✓ handles a click

Finished in 0.046 secs / 0.014 secs @ 16:23:18 GMT-0500 (Colombia Standard Time)

SUMMARY:
✓ 4 tests completed
```

Figure 8-3. *Running tests*

You can generate docs by executing $ npm run docs.

And with $npm run docs:serve, you can see the documentation created.

These tasks use eleventy, a static site generator, to generate beautiful documentation, depending on the templates that we create in the folder docs-src (Figure 8-4).

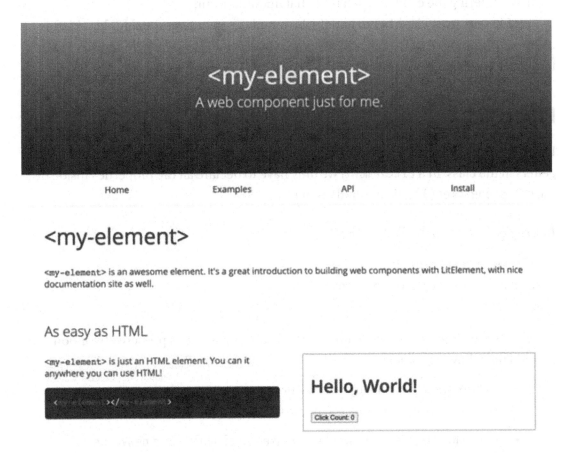

Figure 8-4. *Running docs*

As you see, this starter is a good starting point for building our components. In the next sections, we are going to migrate <simple-form-modal-component>, <note-list-component>, and <note-list-item-component>, using a new project for each web component.

LitElement

LitElement is a library that gives us a base class for creating web components without worrying about having to take care of low-level complexity when we are using only JS, such as rendering the element each time that updates occur.

LitElement uses lit-html to handle the templates in our component. lit-html is a templating library that we can add in our JS projects independently, to render HTML templates with data efficiently.

Properties

In the previous chapters, you may remember that we created properties with setters and getters in the class. In a LitElement, we only have to declare all the properties inside of the get properties() static method, as in Listing 8-1.

Listing 8-1. Declaring Properties

```
static get properties() {
  return { propertyName: options};
}
```

LitElement is going to handle updates and conversion for us properly. In options, we can add the following values:

- Attribute: This value indicates whether the property is associated with an attribute or a custom name for the associated attribute.

- hasChanged: This is a function that takes an oldValue and newValue and returns a Boolean to indicate whether a property has changed when being set.

- Type: This is a type of hint for converting between properties and attributes. You can use String, Number, Boolean, Array, Object.

An example of declaring properties in <simple-form-modal-component> is given in Listing 8-2.

Listing 8-2. Declaring Properties in `<simple-form-modal-component>`

```
static get properties() {
    return {
      open: {
        type: Boolean,
        hasChanged(newVal, oldVal) {
          if (oldVal !== newVal) {
            return true;
          }
          else {
            return false;
          }
        }
      }
    };
}
```

Here, we are creating the open property as `Boolean` and checking the logic when the property changes. You can find all the mechanisms for properties at `https://lit-element.polymer-project.org/guide/properties`.

Templates

Rendering and updating the DOM when changes occur is a difficult task, and this can affect the performance of the code in the functions that handle this. `lit-html` tackles this complexity and gives us a comfortable way to build our templates.

Using templates is simple: just use the `render()` method in the component and return a template literal with the `html` tag function, as in Listing 8-3.

Listing 8-3. Using Templates

```
import { LitElement, html } from 'lit-element';
class MyComponent extends LitElement {
  render(){
    return html`
      <div>
        My Component content
      </div>
    `;
  }
}
customElements.define('my-component, MyComponent);
```

If we have to use a property, we must call it inside the template literal, with the `this.` prop notation, as in Listing 8-4.

Listing 8-4. Using a Property in Templates

```
import { LitElement, html } from 'lit-element';
class MyComponent extends LitElement {
static get properties() {
    return {
      myString: { type: String }
    };
  }
  render(){
    return html`
      <div>
        My Component content with ${this.myString}
      </div>
    `;
  }
}
customElements.define('my-component, MyComponent);
```

If we want to bind an attribute, we can pass it directly from the template literal, as in Listing 8-5.

Listing 8-5. Binding an Attribute in Templates

```
import { LitElement, html } from 'lit-element';
class MyComponent extends LitElement {
static get properties() {
    return {
      myId: { type: String }
    };
  }
  render(){
    return html`
      <div id="${this.myId}">
        My Component content
      </div>
    `;
  }
}
```

If we want to bind a property, we can pass it with `.prop` notation from the template literal, as in Listing 8-6.

Listing 8-6. Binding a Property in Templates

```
import { LitElement, html } from 'lit-element';
class MyComponent extends LitElement {
static get properties() {
    return {
      myValue: { type: String }
    };
  }
  render(){
    return html`
      <input type="checkbox" .value="${this.myValue}"/>
    `;
  }
}
```

If we want to bind a clickHandler to a click event, we can pass it with the $click notation from the template literal, as in Listing 8-7.

Listing 8-7. Binding a clickHandler in a Click Event

```
import { LitElement, html } from 'lit-element';
class MyComponent extends LitElement {
  render(){
    return html`
      <button @click="${this.clickHandler}">click</button>
    `;
  }
  clickHandler(e) {
    console.log(e.target);
  }
}
```

You can find all the mechanisms for templates at https://lit-element.polymer-project.org/guide/templates or https://lit-html.polymer-project.org/guide.

Styles

Adding styles in your web components with Polymer is straightforward. Simply add your selectors and properties in the static method styles(), as in Listing 8-8.

Listing 8-8. Adding Styles in Web Components

```
import { LitElement, html } from 'lit-element';

class MyComponent extends LitElement {
  static get styles() {
    return css`
      div { color: blue; }
    `;
  }
```

```
render() {
  return html`
    <div>Content in Blue!</div>
   `;
}}
```

You can read more about styles at https://lit-element.polymer-project.org/ guide/styles.

Events

You can add events listeners directly in your template, as in Listing 8-9.

Listing 8-9. Adding an Event in the Template

```
import { LitElement, html } from 'lit-element';
class MyComponent extends LitElement {

  render() {
    return html`<button @click="${this.handleEvent}">click</button>`;
  }

  handleEvent(e) {
   console.log(e);
  }
}
```

You can also add the listener directly in the component, in some method of the life cycle, as in Listing 8-10.

Listing 8-10. Adding an Event in the Component

```
import { LitElement, html } from 'lit-element';

class MyComponent extends LitElement {

  constructor() {
    super();
    this.addEventListener('DOMContentLoaded', this.handleEvent);
  }
```

```
handleEvent() {
  console.log('It is Loaded');
 }
}
```

You can read more about events at https://lit-element.polymer-project.org/ guide/events.

Life Cycle

LitElement inherits the default life cycle callbacks from the Web Components standard and some additional methods that can be used to add logic in our components.

> connectedCallback: This is invoked when a component is added to the document's DOM (Listing 8-11).

Listing 8-11. connectedCallback

```
import { LitElement, html } from 'lit-element';

class MyComponent extends LitElement {

  connectedCallback() {
    super.connectedCallback();
    console.log('added');
  }
}
```

> disconnectedCallback: This is invoked when a component is removed from the document's DOM (Listing 8-12).

Listing 8-12. disconnectedCallback

```
import { LitElement, html } from 'lit-element';

class MyComponent extends LitElement {

  disconnectedCallback() {
    super.disconnectedCallback();
```

```
    console.log('removed');
  }
}
```

adoptedCallback: This is invoked when a component is moved to a new document (Listing 8-13).

Listing 8-13. adoptedCallback

```
import { LitElement, html } from 'lit-element';

class MyComponent extends LitElement {

  adoptedCallback() {
    super.disconnectedCallback();
    console.log('moved');
  }
}
```

attibuteChangedCallback: This is invoked when a component attribute changes (Listing 8-14).

Listing 8-14. attibuteChangedCallback

```
import { LitElement, html } from 'lit-element';

class MyComponent extends LitElement {

  attributeChangedCallback(name, oldVal, newVal) {
    super.attributeChangedCallback(name, oldVal, newVal);
    console.log('attribute change: ', name, newVal);
  }
}
```

firstUpdated: This is invoked after the first time your component has been updated and rendered (Listing 8-15).

Listing 8-15. `firstUpdated`

```
import { LitElement, html } from 'lit-element';

class MyComponent extends LitElement {

  firstUpdated(changedProperties) {
    console.log('first updated');
  }
}
```

> updated: This is invoked when the element's DOM has been
> updated and rendered (Listing 8-16).

Listing 8-16. `updated`

```
import { LitElement, html } from 'lit-element';

class MyComponent extends LitElement {

  updated(changedProperties) {
    changedProperties.forEach((oldValue, propName) => {
      console.log(`${propName} changed. oldValue: ${oldValue}`);
    });
  }
}
```

You can read more about the life cycle in `https://lit-element.polymer-project.org/guide/lifecycle`.

Building with Polymer

In this section, we are going to build our `<simple-form-modal-component>`, `<note-list-component>`, and `<note-list-item-component>`, using the Polymer starter.

As you see in Listing 8-17, we have our `SimpleFormModalComponent` in VanillaJS.

Listing 8-17. SimpleFormModalComponent in VanillaJS

```
export class SimpleFormModalComponent extends HTMLElement {

  constructor() {
      super();

      this.root = this.attachShadow({mode: 'open'});
      this.container = document.createElement('div');
      this.container.innerHTML = this.getTemplate();
      this.root.appendChild(this.container.cloneNode(true));

      this._open = this.getAttribute('open') || false;

      this.modal = this.root.getElementById("myModal");
      this.addBtn = this.root.getElementById("addBtn");
      this.closeBtn = this.root.getElementById("closeBtn");

      this.handleAdd = this.handleAdd.bind(this);
      this.handleCancel = this.handleCancel.bind(this);

  }
  connectedCallback() {
    this.addBtn.addEventListener('click', this.handleAdd);
    this.closeBtn.addEventListener('click', this.handleCancel);
  }

  disconnectedCallback () {
    this.addBtn.removeEventListener('click', this.handleAdd);
    this.closeBtn.removeEventListener('click', this.handleCancel);
  }

  get open() {
    return this._open;
  }

  set open(newValue) {
    this._open = newValue;
    this.showModal(this._open);
  }
```

```
handleAdd() {
  const fTitle = this.root.getElementById('ftitle');
  const fDesc = this.root.getElementById('fdesc');
  this.dispatchEvent(new CustomEvent('add-event', {bubbles: true,
  composed:true, detail: {title: fTitle.value, description: fDesc.
  value}}));

  fTitle.value = '';
  fDesc.value = '';
  this.open = false;
}

handleCancel() {
  this.open = false;
}

showModal(state) {
  if(state) {
    this.modal.style.display = "block";
  } else {
    this.modal.style.display = "none"
  }
}

getTemplate() {
    return `
    ${this.getStyle()}
    <div id="myModal" class="modal">
      <div class="modal-content">
        <form id="myForm">
          <label for="ftitle">Title:</label><br>
          <input type="text" id="ftitle" name="ftitle"><br>
          <label for="fdesc">Description:</label><br>
          <textarea id="fdesc" name="fdesc" rows="4" cols="50">
          </textarea><br/>
          <button type="button" id="addBtn">Add</button><button type=
          "button" id="closeBtn">Close</button>
```

```
          </form>
        </div>
      </div>`;
  }

  getStyle() {
      return `
      <style>
        .modal {
          display: none;
          position: fixed;
          z-index: 1;
          padding-top: 100px;
          left: 0;
          top: 0;
          width: 100%;
          height: 100%;
          overflow: auto;
          background-color: rgb(0,0,0);
          background-color: rgba(0,0,0,0.4);
        }
        .modal-content {
          background-color: #fefefe;
          margin: auto;
          padding: 20px;
          border: 1px solid #888;
          width: 50%;
        }
      </style>`;
  }
}
customElements.define('simple-form-modal-component',
SimpleFormModalComponent);
```

We have a getTemplate() method that returns the HTML for our component, a getStyle() method that returns the styles rules that we are using inside the component, some methods that we are adding in the component to handle some logic in the component, and some setter and getters that update the properties in the component. We can use the same principles to create a LitElement quickly and make our code shorter, because LitElement handles some low-level things for us.

We can start with the properties using the LitElement syntax, as in Listing 8-18.

Listing 8-18. Adding Properties in SimpleFormModalComponent with LitElement

```
import {LitElement, html, css} from 'lit-element';

export class SimpleFormModalComponent extends LitElement {
static get properties() {
    return {
      open: {
        type: Boolean
      }
    };
  }

  constructor() {
    super();
    this.open = false;
  }
}

window.customElements.define('simple-form-modal-component',
SimpleFormModalComponent);
```

Here, we are adding our 'open' property as a Boolean, and we are initializing this property as false in the constructor().

Next, we are going to take the method getTemplate() and migrate in LitElement, as in Listing 8-19.

Listing 8-19. Adding render() in SimpleFormModalComponent with LitElement

```
import {LitElement, html, css} from 'lit-element';

export class SimpleFormModalComponent extends LitElement {
static get properties() {
    return {
      open: {
        type: Boolean
      }
    };
  }

  constructor() {
    super();
    this.open = false;
  }

  render() {
    return html`
      <div id="myModal" class="modal">
        <div class="modal-content">
          <form id="myForm">
            <label for="ftitle">Title:</label><br>
            <input type="text" id="ftitle" name="ftitle"><br>
            <label for="fdesc">Description:</label><br>
            <textarea id="fdesc" name="fdesc" rows="4" cols="50">
            </textarea><br/>
            <button type="button" id="addBtn">Add</button>
            <button type="button" id="closeBtn">Close</button>
          </form>
        </div>
      </div>
    `;
  }
}

window.customElements.define('simple-form-modal-component',
SimpleFormModalComponent);
```

As you can see, it is almost the same code, but we are using the render() method and return an HTML tag literal instead of a string.

Now we are going to do the same with getStyle(), moving this to the styles() getter, as in Listing 8-20.

Listing 8-20. Adding render() in SimpleFormModalComponent with LitElement

```
import {LitElement, html, css} from 'lit-element';

export class SimpleFormModalComponent extends LitElement {
static get styles() {
    return css`
      .modal {
        display: none;
        position: fixed;
        z-index: 1;
        padding-top: 100px;
        left: 0;
        top: 0;
        width: 100%;
        height: 100%;
        overflow: auto;
        background-color: rgb(0,0,0);
        background-color: rgba(0,0,0,0.4);
      }
      .modal-content {
        background-color: #fefefe;
        margin: auto;
        padding: 20px;
        border: 1px solid #888;
        width: 50%;
      }
    `;
}
```

```
static get properties() {
    return {
      open: {
        type: Boolean
      }
    };
  }

  constructor() {
    super();
    this.open = false;
  }

  render() {
    return html`
      <div id="myModal" class="modal">
        <div class="modal-content">
          <form id="myForm">
            <label for="ftitle">Title:</label><br>
            <input type="text" id="ftitle" name="ftitle"><br>
            <label for="fdesc">Description:</label><br>
            <textarea id="fdesc" name="fdesc" rows="4" cols="50">
            </textarea><br/>
            <button type="button" id="addBtn">Add</button>
            <button type="button" id="closeBtn">Close</button>
          </form>
        </div>
      </div>
    `;
  }
}

window.customElements.define('simple-form-modal-component',
SimpleFormModalComponent);
```

Now we are going to add the handler methods for the button, using the @click notation, as in Listing 8-21.

Listing 8-21. Adding styles() in SimpleFormModalComponent with LitElement

```
import {LitElement, html, css} from 'lit-element';

export class SimpleFormModalComponent extends LitElement {
static get styles() {
    return css`
      .modal {
        display: none;
        position: fixed;
        z-index: 1;
        padding-top: 100px;
        left: 0;
        top: 0;
        width: 100%;
        height: 100%;
        overflow: auto;
        background-color: rgb(0,0,0);
        background-color: rgba(0,0,0,0.4);
      }
      .modal-content {
        background-color: #fefefe;
        margin: auto;
        padding: 20px;
        border: 1px solid #888;
        width: 50%;
      }
    `;
}

static get properties() {
    return {
      open: {
        type: Boolean
      }
    };
  }
```

```
constructor() {
  super();
  this.open = false;
}

render() {
  return html`
    <div id="myModal" class="modal">
      <div class="modal-content">
        <form id="myForm">
          <label for="ftitle">Title:</label><br>
          <input type="text" id="ftitle" name="ftitle"><br>
          <label for="fdesc">Description:</label><br>
          <textarea id="fdesc" name="fdesc" rows="4" cols="50">
          </textarea><br/>
          <button type="button" id="addBtn" @click=${this.handleAdd}>
          Add</button>
          <button type="button" id="closeBtn" @click=${this.handle
          Cancel}>Close</button>
        </form>
      </div>
    </div>
  `;
}

handleAdd() {
  const fTitle = this.shadowRoot.getElementById('ftitle');
  const fDesc = this.shadowRoot.getElementById('fdesc');
  this.dispatchEvent(new CustomEvent('addEvent', {detail: {title: fTitle.
  value, description: fDesc.value}}));

  fTitle.value = '';
  fDesc.value = '';
  this.open = false;
}
```

```
handleCancel() {
  this.open = false;
  }
}
window.customElements.define('simple-form-modal-component',
SimpleFormModalComponent);
```

Finally, we are going to add the showModal() method for when 'open' is updated, as in Listing 8-22.

Listing 8-22. Adding render() in SimpleFormModalComponent with LitElement

```
import {LitElement, html, css} from 'lit-element';

export class SimpleFormModalComponent extends LitElement {
  static get styles() {
    return css`
      .modal {
        display: none;
        position: fixed;
        z-index: 1;
        padding-top: 100px;
        left: 0;
        top: 0;
        width: 100%;
        height: 100%;
        overflow: auto;
        background-color: rgb(0,0,0);
        background-color: rgba(0,0,0,0.4);
      }
      .modal-content {
        background-color: #fefefe;
        margin: auto;
        padding: 20px;
        border: 1px solid #888;
        width: 50%;
      }
```

```
      `;
}

static get properties() {
  return {
    open: {
      type: Boolean,
      hasChanged(newVal, oldVal) {
        if (oldVal !== newVal) {
          return true;
        }
        else {
          return false;
        }
      }
    }
  };
}

constructor() {
  super();
  this.open = false;
}

render() {
  return html`
    <div id="myModal" class="modal">
      <div class="modal-content">
        <form id="myForm">
          <label for="ftitle">Title:</label><br>
          <input type="text" id="ftitle" name="ftitle"><br>
          <label for="fdesc">Description:</label><br>
          <textarea id="fdesc" name="fdesc" rows="4" cols="50">
          </textarea><br/>
          <button type="button" id="addBtn" @click=${this.handleAdd}>
          Add</button>
```

```
              <button type="button" id="closeBtn" @click=${this.
              handleCancel}>Close</button>
          </form>
        </div>
      </div>
    `;
  }

  handleAdd() {
    const fTitle = this.shadowRoot.getElementById('ftitle');
    const fDesc = this.shadowRoot.getElementById('fdesc');
    this.dispatchEvent(new CustomEvent('addEvent', {detail: {title: fTitle.
    value, description: fDesc.value}}));

    fTitle.value = '';
    fDesc.value = '';
    this.open = false;
  }

  handleCancel() {
    this.open = false;
  }

  showModal(state) {
    const modal = this.shadowRoot.getElementById("myModal");
    if(state) {
      modal.style.display = "block";
    } else {
      modal.style.display = "none"
    }
  }

  updated(){
    this.showModal(this.open);
  }
}

window.customElements.define('simple-form-modal-component',
SimpleFormModalComponent);
```

Here, we are using the option hasChanged() in 'open' to check when an update is triggered, and with the updated() method, we use the method showModal() to show/hide the modal. Now, our <simple-form-modal-component> is ready.

You can access the code for this book (https://github.com/carlosrojaso/apress-book-web-components) with

```
$git checkout chap-8.
```

I created an example in the dev/ folder, documentation in the docs-src/ folder, and some basic tests in the test/ folder, then you can run the following:

```
$ npm install
```

```
$ npm run serve
```

To see the example running in localhost:8080/dev, run

```
$ npm run docs
```

```
$ npm run docs:serve
```

We will continue with the <note-list-component> that we wrote in the previous chapters, as in Listing 8-23.

Listing 8-23. NoteListComponent in VanillaJS

```
export class NoteListComponent extends HTMLElement {
  static get observedAttributes() { return ['notes']; }

  constructor() {
    super();

    this._notes = JSON.parse(this.getAttribute('notes')) || [];
    this.root = this.attachShadow({mode: 'open'});
    this.root.innerHTML = this.render();

    this.handleDelEvent = this.handleDelEvent.bind(this);
  }

  attributeChangedCallback(name, oldValue, newValue) {
    switch(name) {
      case 'notes':
```

```
        this.note = JSON.parse(newValue);
        this.root.innerHTML = this.render();
        break;
    }
}

connectedCallback() {
    this.root.addEventListener('del-event', this.handleDelEvent);
}

disconnectedCallback () {
    this.root.removeEventListener('del-event', this.handleDelEvent);
}

handleDelEvent(e) {
    this._notes.splice(e.detail.idx, 1);
    this.root.innerHTML = this.render();
}

render() {
    let noteElements = '';
    this._notes.map(
        (note, idx) => {
            noteElements += `
            <note-list-item-component note='${JSON.stringify(note)}'
            idx='${idx}'></note-list-item-component>`;
        }
    );
    return `
        ${noteElements}`;
}
get notes(){
    return this._notes;
}
```

```
  set notes(newValue) {
    this._notes = newValue;
    this.root.innerHTML = this.render();
  }
}
customElements.define('note-list-component', NoteListComponent);
```

We are going to add the properties for the component, per Listing 8-24.

Listing 8-24. Adding Properties in `NoteListComponent` with `LitElement`

```
import {LitElement, html, css} from 'lit-element';

export class NoteListComponent extends LitElement {
static get properties() {
    return {
      notes: {
        type: Array,
        attribute: true,
        reflect: true,
      }
    };
  }

  constructor() {
    super();
    this.notes = this.getAttribute("notes") || [];
  }
}
```

Here, we are defining our notes property as an array and adding the `options` attribute to make the property work correctly as an attribute. In the `constructor()`, we are initializing `this.notes` with the value in `'notes'` or an empty array.

Now we are going to migrate the `render()` method, which is similar to a `LitElement`, as you can see in Listing 8-25.

Listing 8-25. Adding a Template in NoteListComponent with LitElement

```
import {LitElement, html, css} from 'lit-element';

export class NoteListComponent extends LitElement {
static get properties() {
    return {
      notes: {
        type: Array,
        attribute: true,
        reflect: true,
      }
    };
  }

  constructor() {
    super();
    this.notes = this.getAttribute("notes") || [];
  }

  render() {
    return html`
      ${this.notes.map((note, idx) => {
        return html` <note-list-item-component
          note="${JSON.stringify(note)}"
          idx="${idx}"
        ></note-list-item-component>`;
      })}
    `;
  }
}
```

Here, we are using map() to iterate in notes and returning all as an HTML tag literal, to make our template work correctly.

We must update notes each time that the value changes, but to do this, we must do something special, because when passed as a reference, the hasChanged() option doesn't detect when a change in the array is occurring. To fix this, we are going to use attributeChangedCallback(), as in Listing 8-26.

Listing 8-26. Adding attributeChangedCallback in NoteListComponent with LitElement

```
import {LitElement, html, css} from 'lit-element';

export class NoteListComponent extends LitElement {
static get properties() {
    return {
      notes: {
        type: Array,
        attribute: true,
        reflect: true,
      }
    };
  }

  constructor() {
    super();
    this.notes = this.getAttribute("notes") || [];
  }

  attributeChangedCallback() {
    this.notes = [...this.notes];
    super.attributeChangedCallback();
  }

  render() {
    return html`
      ${this.notes.map((note, idx) => {
        return html` <note-list-item-component
          note="${JSON.stringify(note)}"
          idx="${idx}"
        ></note-list-item-component>`;
      })}
    `;
  }
}
```

Here, in `attributeChangedCallback()`, we are detecting a change in the component. If it is occurring, we can update `this.notes` with a new array (not a reference), using the spread operator, and with this small fix, our component is going to work correctly again.

Finally, we are going to add the event listener for `'del-event'` and the `handleDelEvent()` function, as in Listing 8-27. With these modifications, our component is ready.

Listing 8-27. Adding the Event Listener in `NoteListComponent` with `LitElement`

```
import {LitElement, html, css} from 'lit-element';

export class NoteListComponent extends LitElement {
static get properties() {
    return {
      notes: {
        type: Array,
        attribute: true,
        reflect: true,
      }
    };
  }

  constructor() {
    super();
    this.notes = this.getAttribute("notes") || [];
    this.addEventListener("del-event", this.handleDelEvent);
  }

  attributeChangedCallback() {
    this.notes = [...this.notes];
    super.attributeChangedCallback();
  }

  handleDelEvent(e) {
    this.notes.splice(e.detail.idx, 1);
    this.requestUpdate();
  }
```

```
render() {
  return html`
    ${this.notes.map((note, idx) => {
      return html` <note-list-item-component
        note="${JSON.stringify(note)}"
        idx="${idx}"
      ></note-list-item-component>`;
    })}
  `;
}
}
```

You can access the code for this book (https://github.com/carlosrojaso/apress-book-web-components) at $git checkout chap-8-1.

I created an example in the dev/ folder, documentation in the docs-src/ folder, and some basic tests in the test/ folder, then you can run the following:

$ npm install

$ npm run serve

To see the example running in localhost:8080/dev, run the following:

$ npm run docs

$ npm run docs:serve

Now we are going to migrate our last component, <note-list-item-component>, which we wrote in the previous chapters (see Listing 8-28).

Listing 8-28. NoteListComponent in VanillaJS

```
export class NoteListItemComponent extends HTMLElement {
  static get observedAttributes() { return ['note', 'idx']; }

  constructor() {
    super();

    this._note = JSON.parse(this.getAttribute('note')) || {};
    this.idx = this.getAttribute('idx') || -1;
```

```
    this.root = this.attachShadow({mode: 'open'});
    this.root.innerHTML = this.getTemplate();

    this.delBtn = this.root.getElementById('deleteButton');
    this.handleDelete = this.handleDelete.bind(this);
  }
  connectedCallback() {
    this.delBtn.addEventListener('click', this.handleDelete);
  }

  disconnectedCallback () {
    this.delBtn.removeEventListener('click', this.handleDelete);
  }

  attributeChangedCallback(name, oldValue, newValue) {
    switch(name) {
      case 'note':
        this.note = JSON.parse(newValue);
        this.handleUpdate();
        break;
      case 'idx':
        this.idx = newValue;
        this.handleUpdate();
        break;
    }
  }

  get note() {
    return this._note;
  }

  set note(newValue) {
    this._note = newValue;
  }

  get idx() {
    return this._idx;
  }
```

```
set idx(newValue) {
  this._idx = newValue;
}

handleDelete() {
  this.dispatchEvent(new CustomEvent('del-event', {bubbles:
  true,  composed: true, detail: {idx: this.idx}}));
}

handleUpdate() {
  this.root.innerHTML = this.getTemplate();
  this.delBtn = this.root.getElementById('deleteButton');
  this.handleDelete = this.handleDelete.bind(this);
  this.delBtn.addEventListener('click', this.handleDelete);
 }

getStyle() {
  return `
  <style>
    .note {
      background-color: #ffffcc;
      border-left: 6px solid #ffeb3b;
    }
    div {
      margin: 5px 0px 5px;
      padding: 4px 12px;
    }
  </style>
  `;
}

getTemplate() {
  return`
  ${this.getStyle()}
  <div class="note">
    <p><strong>${this._note.title}</strong> ${this._note.description}
    </p><br/>
```

```
    <button type="button" id="deleteButton">Delete</button>
  </div>`;
  }
}
customElements.define('note-list-item-component', NoteListItemComponent);
```

The process to migrate this component is similar to the steps that we followed before. Therefore, I'll skip the explanation and just show you the complete component in LitElement (Listing 8-29).

Listing 8-29. NoteListItemComponent with LitElement

```
import { LitElement, html, css } from "lit-element";

/**
 * A Note List Item Component
 */
export class NoteListItemComponent extends LitElement {
  static get properties() {
    return {
      /**
       * The attribute is an Object.
       */
      note: {
        type: Object,
        attribute: true,
        reflect: true,
      },
      /**
       * The attribute is a number.
       */
      idx: {
        type: Number,
        attribute: true,
        reflect: true,
      }
    };
  }
```

```
static get styles() {
  return css`
    .note {
      background-color: #ffffcc;
      border-left: 6px solid #ffeb3b;
    }

    div {
      margin: 5px 0px 5px;
      padding: 4px 12px;
    }
  `;
}

constructor() {
  super();
  this.note = JSON.parse(this.getAttribute('note')) || {};
  this.idx = this.getAttribute('idx') || -1;
}

render() {
  return html`
  <div class="note">
    <p><strong>${this.note.title}</strong> ${this.note.description}
    </p><br/>
    <button type="button" id="deleteButton" @click="${this.
    handleDelete}">Delete</button>
  </div>
  `;
}

handleDelete() {
  this.dispatchEvent(new CustomEvent('del-event', {bubbles:
  true,  composed: true, detail: {idx: this.idx}}));
}
}
```

```
window.customElements.define('note-list-item-component',
NoteListItemComponent);
```

You can access the code for this book (`https://github.com/carlosrojaso/apress-book-web-components`) at `$git checkout chap-8-2`.

Awesome! We now have all our components in Polymer as `LitElements`.

Summary

In this chapter, you learned

- How to use `LitElement` and `lit-html` in our components

- How to migrate components from VanillaJS to Polymer

- What the main features of `litElement` are

CHAPTER 9

Working with Vue.js

Vue.js is an open source, progressive JavaScript framework for building user interfaces that aim to be incrementally adoptable. The core library of Vue.js is focused on the view layer only and is easy to pick up and integrate with other libraries or existing projects.

You'll learn to take advantage of its features to build fast, high-performance web apps. Throughout this chapter, we are going to develop an app, and you will learn some key concepts and understand how to integrate Web Components and Vue.js.

What Are the Major Features of Vue.js?

Vue.js has all the features a framework to build single-page applications should have. Some features stand out above the others, such as the following:

- *Virtual DOM*: Virtual DOM is a lightweight in-memory tree representation of the original HTML DOM that can be updated without affecting the original DOM.

- *Components*: These are used to create reusable custom elements in Vue.js applications.

- *Templates*: Vue.js provides HTML-based templates that bind the DOM with the Vue instance data.

- *Routing*: Navigation between pages is achieved through `vue-router`.

- *Lightweight*: Vue.js is a lightweight library compared to other frameworks.

139

© Carlos Rojas 2021
C. Rojas, *Building Native Web Components*, https://doi.org/10.1007/978-1-4842-5905-4_9

What Are Components in Vue.js?

Components are reusable elements with which we define their names and behavior. To understand this concept, look at Figure 9-1.

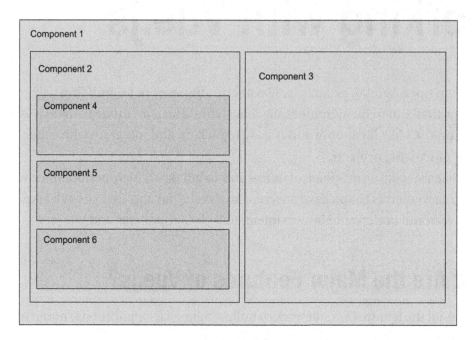

Figure 9-1. *Components in a web application*

You can see in Figure 9-1 that we have six components at different levels. Component 1 is the parent of Component 2 and Component 3, and the grandparent of Component 4, Component 5, and Component 6. Therefore, we can make a hierarchical tree to express this relationship (Figure 9-2).

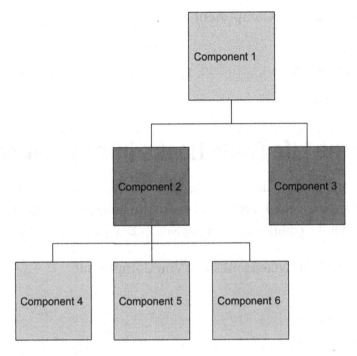

Figure 9-2. *Hierarchy of components*

Now, think that each component can be what we want—a list, an image, a button, text, or whatever we define. The fundamental way to define a simple Vue's component is shown in Listing 9-1.

Listing 9-1. Declaring a Vue's Component

```
const app = createApp({...})
app.component('my-button', {
  data: function () {
    return {
      counter: 0
    }
  },
  template: '<button v-on:click="counter++">Clicks {{ counter }}.</button>'
})}
```

We can add this in our app as a new HTML tag, as in Listing 9-2.

Listing 9-2. Using a Vue's Component

```
<div id="app">
  <my-button></my-button>
</div>
```

What Are the Life Cycle Hooks in Vue Components?

Components are created and destroyed. Collectively, these processes are known as a life cycle, and there are some methods we can use to run functions at specific moments of that cycle. Consider the component that appears in Listing 9-3.

Listing 9-3. Using Life Cycle Hooks in a Vue Component

```
<script>
export default {
  name: 'HelloWorld',
  created: function () {
    console.log('Component created.');
  },
  mounted: function() {
    fetch('https://randomuser.me/api/?results=1')
    .then(
      (response) => {
        return response.json();
      }
    )
    .then(
      (reponseObject) => {
        this.email = reponseObject.results[0].email;
      }
    );
    console.log('Component is mounted.');
  },
```

```
  props: {
    msg: String,
    email:String
  }
}
</script>
```

Here, we are adding an email property with the methods created() and mounted(). These methods are called *life cycle hooks*. We are going to use these to perform actions at specific moments in our component, for example, when we are making a call to an API when our component is mounted and getting the email at that moment.

Life cycle hooks are an essential part of any serious Vue component (see Figure 9-3).

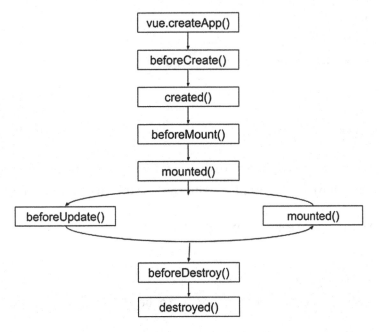

Figure 9-3. *Life cycle of a Vue component*

beforeCreate

The beforeCreate hook runs at the early initialization of your component. You can use this method as in Listing 9-4.

Listing 9-4. Using beforeCreate in a Vue Component

```
Vue.createApp({
  beforeCreate: function () {
    console.log('Initialization is happening');
})
```

created

The created hook runs when your component is initialized. You will be able to access reactive data, and events are active. You can use this method as in Listing 9-5.

Listing 9-5. Using created in a Vue Component

```
Vue.createApp({
  created: function () {
    console.log('The Component is created');
})
```

beforeMount

The beforeMount hook runs right before the initial render occurs and after the template or render functions have been compiled. You can use this method as in Listing 9-6.

Listing 9-6. Using beforeMount in a Vue Component

```
Vue.createApp({
  beforeMount: function () {
    console.log('The component is going to be Mounted');
  }
})
```

mounted

The mounted hook provides full access to the reactive component, templates, and rendered DOM (via. this.$el). You can use this method as in Listing 9-7.

Listing 9-7. Using mounted in a Vue Component

```
Vue.createApp({
  mounted: function () {
    console.log('The component is mounted');
  }
})
```

beforeUpdate

The beforeUpdate hook runs after data changes on your component and the update cycle begins, right before the DOM is patched and re-rendered. You can use this method as in Listing 9-8.

Listing 9-8. Using beforeUpdate in a Vue Component

```
Vue.createApp({
  beforeUpdate: function () {
    console.log('The component is going to be updated');
  }
})
```

updated

The updated hook runs after data changes on your component and the DOM re-renders. You can use this method as in Listing 9-9.

Listing 9-9. Using updated in a Vue Component

```
Vue.createApp({
  updated: function () {
    console.log('The component is updated');
  }
})
```

beforeDestroy

The beforeDestroy hook is called right before the component is destroyed. Your component will still be fully present and functional. You can use this method as in Listing 9-10.

Listing 9-10. Using beforeDestroy in a Vue Component

```
Vue.createApp({
  beforeDestroy: function () {
    console.log('The component is going to be destroyed');
  }
})
```

destroyed

The destroyed hook is called when everything that was attached to it has been destroyed. You might use the destroyed hook to perform any last-minute cleanup. You can use this method as in Listing 9-11.

Listing 9-11. Using destroyed in a Vue Component

```
Vue.createApp({
  destroyed: function () {
    console.log('The component is destroyed');
  }
})
```

Communicating Between Vue Components

Components must usually share information between them. For these basic scenarios, we can use props or ref attributes, if you want to pass data to child components; emitters, if you're going to pass data to a parent component; and two-way data binding, to have data sync between child and parents (see Figure 9-4).

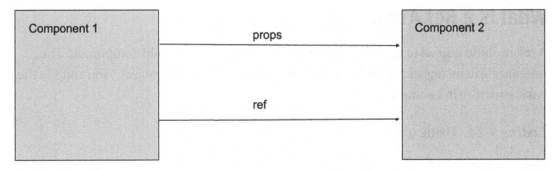

Figure 9-4. *Communicatiion between a parent component and a child component*

As you can see in Figure 9-4, if you want a parent component to communicate with a child component, you can use props or a ref attribute.

What Are Props?

Props are custom attributes that you can register on a component. When a value is passed to a prop attribute, it becomes a property on that component's instance. You can see the basic structure in Listing 9-12.

Listing 9-12. Declaring Props in a Vue Component

```
const app = createApp({...})
app.component('some-item', {
  props: ['somevalue'],
  template: '<div>{{ somevalue }}</div>'
})
```

Now you can pass values as in Listing 9-13.

Listing 9-13. Using Props in a Vue Component

```
<some-item somevalue="value for prop"></some-item>
```

What Is a Ref Attribute?

A ref attribute is used to register a reference to an element or a child component. The reference will be registered under the parent component's `$refs` object.[1] You can see the basic structure in Listing 9-14.

Listing 9-14. Using a Ref in a Vue Component

```
<input type="text" ref="email">

<script>
    const input = this.$refs.email;
</script>
```

Emitting an Event

If you want to communicate to a child with a parent, you can use `$emit()`, which is the recommended method for passing information. Calling a prop function is an alternative approach to passing information (Figure 9-5) but a bad practice, because it can be confusing when your project is growing, which is why I will skip this.

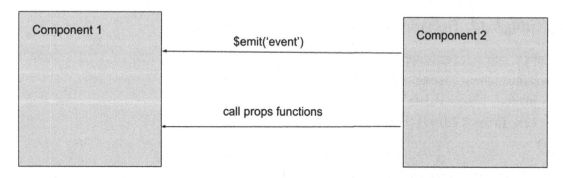

Figure 9-5. *Communicating to a child component with a parent component*

In Vue, the $emit method can be used to send data to parents' components. In Listing 9-15, you can see the basic structure for emitting an event.

---

[1]https://v3.vuejs.org/api/instance-properties.html#refs

Listing 9-15. Using a Ref in a Vue Component

```
const app = createApp({...})
app.component('child-custom-component', {
  data: function () {
    return {
      customValue: 0
    }
  },
  methods: {
    giveValue: function () {
      this.$emit('give-value', this.customValue++)
    }
  },
  template: `
    <button v-on:click="giveValue">
      Click me for value
    </button>
  `
})
```

Using Two-Way Data Binding

One easy way to facilitate communication between components is to use two-way
data binding. In the following scenario, Vue.js makes the communication between
components for us (Figure 9-6).

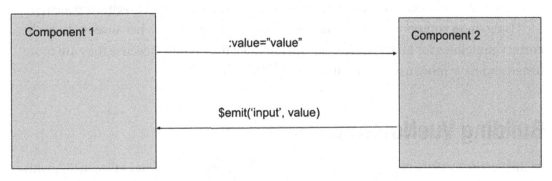

Figure 9-6. *Two-way communication between components*

Two-way data binding means that Vue.js syncs data properties and DOM for you. Changes to a data property update the DOM, and modifications made to the DOM update the data property. So, data moves both ways. In Listing 9-16, you can see the basic structure for using two-way data binding.

Listing 9-16. Using v-model in a Vue Component

```
const app = Vue.createApp({})
app.component('my-component', {
  props: {
    myProp: String
  },
  template: `
    <input
      type="text"
      :value="myProp"
      @input="$emit('update: myProp, $event.target.value)">
    `
})
<my-component v-model:myProp="Some Value"></my-component>
```

Material Web Components

In Chapter 8, we built some web components using VanillaJS and Polymer. This was an excellent means of learning the basics of these technologies. Still, for our VueNoteApp, we are going to use a more robust Web Components catalog, maintained by Google, that implements Material Design and are built using LitElement. You can find these components at https://github.com/material-components/material-components-web-components.

Using these components helps us to increase our productivity, because we have the correct guidelines for Material Design, and enhance the quality, because they are more tested and have more use options in our user interfaces.

Building VueNoteApp

In this section, we are going to build a complete Note App, as shown in Figure 9-7, with Vue, using Material Design.

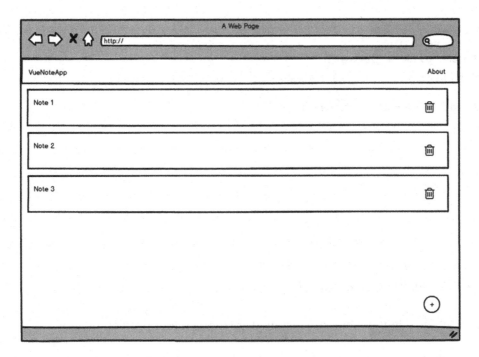

Figure 9-7. *VueNoteApp design*

Creating a New Vue Project

First, we are going to create a new project in Vue 3, using the Vue CLI. Be sure that you are using the latest version of the Vue CLI and run the following:

```
$npm update -g @vue/cli
```

To create the project, run the following in your terminal:

```
$vue create note-app
```

Select Vue 3, as in Figure 9-8.

151

```
● ● ●              Projects — node ~/.nvm/versions/node/v10.16.3/bin/vue create note-app — 66×14
Vue CLI v4.5.0
? Please pick a preset:
  Default ([Vue 2] babel, eslint)
> Default (Vue 3 Preview) ([Vue 3] babel, eslint)
  Manually select features
```

Figure 9-8. *Pick Vue 3 in Vue CLI*

After all the dependencies are installed, go to the folder project.

`$cd note-app`

Adding Material Web Components

First, we are going to install the web components that we are going to use in our app.
Install `mwc-button` (Figure 9-9).

Figure 9-9. `mwc-button` *Component*

Then run the following in your terminal:

`$npm install --save @material/mwc-button`

You can see all its properties at `https://github.com/material-components/`
`material-components-web-components/tree/master/packages/button`.
Install `mwc-dialog` (Figure 9-10).

Figure 9-10. *mwc-dialog Component*

Then run the following in your terminal:

```
$npm install --save @material/mwc-dialog
```

You can see all its properties at https://github.com/material-components/
material-components-web-components/tree/master/packages/dialog.

Install mwc-fab (Figure 9-11).

Figure 9-11. *mwc-fab Component*

Then run the following in your terminal:

```
$npm install --save @material/mwc-fab
```

You can see all its properties at https://github.com/material-components/
material-components-web-components/tree/master/packages/fab.

Install `mwc-icon-button` (Figure 9-12).

Figure 9-12. *`mwc-icon-button` Component*

Then run the following in your terminal:

`$npm install --save @material/mwc-icon-button`

You can see all its properties at `https://github.com/material-components/`
`material-components-web-components/tree/master/packages/icon-button`.
Install `mwc-list` (Figure 9-13).

Note 1
Loren Ipsum

Note 0
Loren Ipsum

Note 2
Loren Ipsum

Figure 9-13. *`mwc-list` Component*

Then run the following in your terminal:

`$npm install --save @material/mwc-list`

You can see all its properties in `https://github.com/material-components/`
`material-components-web-components/tree/master/packages/list`.
Install `mwc-textfield` (Figure 9-14).

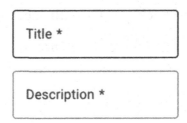

Figure 9-14. `mwc-textfield` *Component*

Then run the following in your terminal:

`$npm install --save @material/mwc-textfield`

You can see all its properties at `https://github.com/material-components/material-components-web-components/tree/master/packages/textfield`.
Install `mwc-top-app-bar` (Figure 9-15).

Login

Figure 9-15. `mwc-top-app-bar` *Component*

Then run the following in your terminal:

`$npm install --save @material/mwc-top-app-bar`

You can see all its properties at `https://github.com/material-components/material-components-web-components/tree/master/packages/top-app-bar`.
Now we are going to install Polyfills to support older web browsers.
Install the following dependencies:

`$npm install --save-dev copy-webpack-plugin @webcomponents/webcomponentsjs`

Add `copy-webpack-plugin` to Vue's Webpack configuration file. To do this, we must create a new file, `vue.config.js`, and add the code in Listing 9-17.

155

Listing 9-17. Using `copy-webpack-plugin` with `webcomponentsjs`

```
const CopyWebpackPlugin = require('copy-webpack-plugin');

module.exports = {
  configureWebpack: {
    plugins: [
      new CopyWebpackPlugin({
        patterns: [{
          context: 'node_modules/@webcomponents/webcomponentsjs',
          from: '**/*.js',
          to: 'webcomponents'
        }]
      })
    ]
  }
};
```

`copy-webpack-plugin` will now copy all the required JS files into a webcomponents directory when building.

Now, in `public/index.html`, we are going to add some lines to check if the web browser supports `customElements` or uses Polyfills (see Listing 9-18).

Listing 9-18. Adding `webcomponentjs` in VueNoteApp

```
<!DOCTYPE html>
<html lang="en">
  <head>
...
    <script src="webcomponents/webcomponents-loader.js"></script>
    <script>
      if (!window.customElements) { document.write('<!--'); }
    </script>
    <script src="webcomponents/custom-elements-es5-adapter.js"></script>
    <!-- ! DO NOT REMOVE THIS COMMENT -->

...
  </body>
</html>
```

In components/HelloWorld.vue, we are going to add mwc-button (see Listing 9-19).

Listing 9-19. Using mwc-button in HelloWorld.vue

```
<template>
  <div class="hello">
    <h1>{{ msg }}</h1>
    <p>
      For a guide and recipes on how to configure / customize this
      project,<br>
      check out the
      <a href="https://cli.vuejs.org" target="_blank" rel="noopener">
      vue-cli documentation</a>.
    </p>
    <h3>Installed CLI Plugins</h3>
    <ul>
      <li><a href="https://github.com/vuejs/vue-cli/tree/dev/packages/
      %40vue/cli-plugin-babel" target="_blank" rel="noopener">babel</a>
      </li>
      <li><a href="https://github.com/vuejs/vue-cli/tree/dev/packages/
      %40vue/cli-plugin-eslint" target="_blank" rel="noopener">eslint
      </a></li>
    </ul>
    <h3>Essential Links</h3>
    <ul>
      <li><a href="https://vuejs.org" target="_blank" rel="noopener">
      Core Docs</a></li>
      <li><a href="https://forum.vuejs.org" target="_blank" rel="noopener">
      Forum</a></li>
      <li><a href="https://chat.vuejs.org" target="_blank" rel="noopener">
      Community Chat</a></li>
      <li><a href="https://twitter.com/vuejs" target="_blank"
      rel="noopener">Twitter</a></li>
      <li><a href="https://news.vuejs.org" target="_blank" rel="noopener">
      News</a></li>
    </ul>
```

```
    <h3>Ecosystem</h3>
    <ul>
      <li><a href="https://router.vuejs.org" target="_blank"
      rel="noopener">vue-router</a></li>
      <li><a href="https://vuex.vuejs.org" target="_blank"
      rel="noopener">vuex</a></li>
      <li><a href="https://github.com/vuejs/vue-devtools#vue-devtools"
      target="_blank" rel="noopener">vue-devtools</a></li>
      <li><a href="https://vue-loader.vuejs.org" target="_blank"
      rel="noopener">vue-loader</a></li>
      <li><a href="https://github.com/vuejs/awesome-vue" target="_blank"
      rel="noopener">awesome-vue</a></li>
    </ul>
    <mwc-button id="myButton" label="Click Me!" @click="handleClick"
    raised></mwc-button>
  </div>
</template>

<script>
import '@material/mwc-button';

export default {
  name: 'HelloWorld',
  props: {
    msg: String
  },
  methods: {
    handleClick() {
      console.log('click');
    }
  },
}
</script>
```

```
<!-- Add "scoped" attribute to limit CSS to this component only -->
<style scoped>
h3 {
  margin: 40px 0 0;
}
ul {
  list-style-type: none;
  padding: 0;
}
li {
  display: inline-block;
  margin: 0 10px;
}
a {
  color: #42b983;
}
</style>
```

To test, run the following:

```
$npm run serve
```

You should see the component in VueNoteApp, as in Figure 9-16.

Welcome to Your Vue.js App

For a guide and recipes on how to configure / customize this project,
check out the vue-cli documentation.

Installed CLI Plugins

babel   eslint

Essential Links

Core Docs   Forum   Community Chat   Twitter   News

Ecosystem

vue-router   vuex   vue-devtools   vue-loader   awesome-vue

CLICK ME!

Figure 9-16. Adding `mwc-button` in `HelloWorld.vue`

You can go there from the GitHub repository at $git checkout v1.0.1.

Adding a Header

We are going to add `mwc-top-app-bar` and create some empty components to organize
our files in a better structure. We must modify `Apps.vue` and add the `mwc-top-app-bar`
component here, as shown in Listing 9-20.

Listing 9-20. Using `mwc-button` in `HelloWorld.vue`

```
<!-- eslint-disable vue/no-deprecated-slot-attribute -->
<template>
  <mwc-top-app-bar centerTitle>
    <mwc-icon-button icon="menu" slot="navigationIcon"></mwc-icon-button>
    <div slot="title">VueNoteApp</div>
    <mwc-icon-button icon="help" slot="actionItems"></mwc-icon-button>
    <div><!-- content --></div>
  </mwc-top-app-bar>
</template>

<script>
import '@material/mwc-top-app-bar';
import '@material/mwc-icon-button';

export default {
  name: 'App',
}
</script>
```

At this point, you can use $npm run serve. The result will look something like Figure 9-17.

Figure 9-17. *Adding* `mwc-top-app-bar`

In addition, we are going to create two empty components, views/Dashboard.vue (see Listing 9-21) and views/About.vue (see Listing 9-22), to allow our app to have different views.

Listing 9-21. `Dashboard.vue`

```
<template>
  <div>
    Dashboard
  </div>
</template>
<script>
export default {
  name: 'Dashboard'
}
</script>
<style>

</style>
```

Listing 9-22. `About.vue`

```
<template>
  <div class="about">
    <h1>This is an about page</h1>
  </div>
</template>
```

You can access this code from GitHub repository at `$git checkout v1.0.2`.

Adding Vue Router

Vue Router is an official routing plug-in for single-page applications, designed for use within the Vue.js framework. A router is a way to jump from one view to another in a single-page application without refreshing the web browser. It is easy to integrate Vue Router in VueNoteApp.

Install the plug-in.

```
$ vue add router
```

Add VueRouter in `main.js`, as in Listing 9-23.

Listing 9-23. Adding Router in `main.js`

```
import { createApp } from 'vue'
import App from './App.vue'
import router from './router'

createApp(App).use(router).mount('#app')
```

Edit the `router/index.js` file and add the router for Dashboard and About, as shown in Listing 9-24.

Listing 9-24. Adding Router in `router/index.js`

```
import { createRouter, createWebHistory } from 'vue-router'
import Dashboard from '../views/Dashboard.vue'
const routes = [
  {
    path: '/',
    name: 'Dashboard',
    component: Dashboard
  },
  {
    path: '/about',
    name: 'About',
    component: () => import(/* webpackChunkName: "about" */ '../views/
    About.vue')
  }
]
const router = createRouter({
  history: createWebHistory(process.env.BASE_URL),
  routes
})

export default router
```

If you look at the /about route, we are using `import()` to load the component. This is because we are loading the component when the user employs that view, instead of loading everything when starting the app. This is called lazy load, and it's good for performance. Now we must add some things in App.vue. The placeholder <router-view> is where the components are going to be loaded, depending on the route, and a <router-link> is a way to change routes in the template (see Listing 9-25).

Listing 9-25. Adding Routes in App.vue

```
<!-- eslint-disable vue/no-deprecated-slot-attribute -->
<template>
  <mwc-top-app-bar centerTitle>
    <div slot="title"><router-link to="/">VueNoteApp</router-link></div>
    <div slot="actionItems"><router-link to="/About">About</router-link>
    </div>
    <div><router-view/></div>
  </mwc-top-app-bar>
</template>

<script>
import '@material/mwc-top-app-bar';
import '@material/mwc-icon-button';

export default {
  name: 'App',
  methods: {
    handleAbout() {
      this.$router.push('About');
    }
  },
}
</script>

<style>
  a, a:visited {
    color:white;
    text-decoration:none;
    padding: 5px;
  }
</style>
```

With these small changes, you should see the header with routes that you can change by pressing on the links, as shown in Figure 9-18.

VueNoteApp   About

This is an about page

Figure 9-18. *Adding routes*

You can access the code from the GitHub repository at $git checkout v1.0.3.

Now we are going to add some elements to views/Dashboard.vue (see Listing 9-26).

Listing 9-26. Adding Web Components in Dashboard.vue

```
<!-- eslint-disable vue/no-deprecated-slot-attribute -->
<template>
  <div>
    <mwc-list multi>
      <mwc-list-item twoline>
        <span>Item 0</span>
        <span slot="secondary">Secondary line</span>
      </mwc-list-item>
      <li divider padded role="separator"></li>
      <mwc-list-item twoline>
        <span>Item 1</span>
        <span slot="secondary">Secondary line</span>
      </mwc-list-item>
      <li divider padded role="separator"></li>
      <mwc-list-item twoline>
        <span>Item 2</span>
        <span slot="secondary">Secondary line</span>
      </mwc-list-item>
```

```
      <li divider padded role="separator"></li>
      <mwc-list-item twoline>
        <span>Item 3</span>
        <span slot="secondary">Secondary line</span>
      </mwc-list-item>
    </mwc-list>
    <mwc-fab class="floatButton" mini icon="add"></mwc-fab>
  </div>
</template>
<script>
import '@material/mwc-list/mwc-list';
import '@material/mwc-list/mwc-list-item';
import '@material/mwc-fab';

export default {
  name: 'Dashboard'
}
</script>
<style scoped>
.floatButton {
  position: fixed;
  bottom: 20px;
  right: 20px;
}
</style>
```

We are adding mwc-list-items to show the notes and an mwc-fab to have a floating button that we are going to use to add new notes.

We are also adding views/About.vue, as shown in Listing 9-27.

Listing 9-27. Adding Routes in About.vue

```
<template>
  <div class="about">
    <h1>Building Native Web Components</h1>
    <h2><i>Front-End Development with Polymer and Vue.js</i></h2>
    <p>
```

Start developing single-page applications (SPAs) with modern architecture. This book shows you how to create, design, and publish native web components, ultimately allowing you to piece together those elements in a modern JavaScript framework.

Building Native Web Components dives right in and gets you started building your first web component. You'll be introduced to native web component design systems and frameworks, discuss component-driven development and understand its importance in large-scale companies. You'll then move on to building web components using templates and APIs, and custom event lifecycles. Techniques and best practices for moving data, customizing, and distributing components are also covered. Throughout, you'll develop a foundation to start using Polymer, Vue.js, and Firebase in your day-to-day work.

Confidently apply modern patterns and develop workflows to build agnostic software pieces that can be reused in SPAs. Building Native Web Components is your guide to developing small and autonomous web components that are focused, independent, reusable, testable, and works with all JavaScript frameworks, modern browsers, and libraries.

```
    </p>
  </div>
</template>
<style scoped>
.about {
  background-color: white;
  text-justify:auto;
  padding: 30px;
}
</style>
```

We are adding some information about the book, and in Figure 9-19 you can see an improvement in appearance that is more in keeping with our goal.

Figure 9-19. *Adding Web Components in* Dashboard.vue

You can access the code from the GitHub the repository at $git checkout v1.0.4.

Deleting a Note

With mwc-list and mws-list-item, we can see our notes in Dashboard.vue in more pleasing fashion, but our notes are static in the code. That is why we are going to create a module in utils/DummyData.js, as in Listing 9-28.

Listing 9-28. DummyData module

```
export const notesData = [
  {id: 1, title: "Note 1", description: "Loren Ipsum"},
  {id: 2, title: "Note 2", description: "Loren Ipsum"},
  {id: 3, title: "Note 3", description: "Loren Ipsum"},
  {id: 4, title: "Note 4", description: "Loren Ipsum"},
  {id: 5, title: "Note 5", description: "Loren Ipsum"},
  {id: 6, title: "Note 6", description: "Loren Ipsum"},
  {id: 7, title: "Note 7", description: "Loren Ipsum"}
];
```

This module is only a simple array with some notes that we can import in Dashboard.vue, but it is handy because now we can load this data dynamically, as in Listing 9-29. In future, we can replace this easily for an API or Firebase.

Listing 9-29. DummyData module

```
<!-- eslint-disable vue/no-deprecated-slot-attribute -->
<template>
  <div>
    <mwc-list v-for="(note) in notes" :key="note.id" multi>
      <mwc-list-item twoline hasMeta>
        <span>{{note.title}}</span>
        <span slot="meta" class="material-icons">delete</span>
        <span slot="secondary">{{note.description}}</span>
      </mwc-list-item>
      <li divider padded role="separator"></li>
    </mwc-list>
    <mwc-fab class="floatButton" mini icon="add"></mwc-fab>
  </div>
</template>
<script>
import '@material/mwc-list/mwc-list';
import '@material/mwc-list/mwc-list-item';
import '@material/mwc-fab';
import '@material/mwc-button';
import { notesData } from '../utils/DummyData';

export default {
  name: 'Dashboard',
  data() {
    return {
      notes: notesData
    }
  }
}
</script>
```

```
<style scoped>
  .floatButton {
    position: fixed;
    bottom: 20px;
    right: 20px;
  }
</style>
```

Now, in Dashboard.vue, we are importing notesData in the property notes, and in the template, we are using directive v-for to iterate in all the notes and create an mwc-list-item for each, as shown in Figure 9-20.

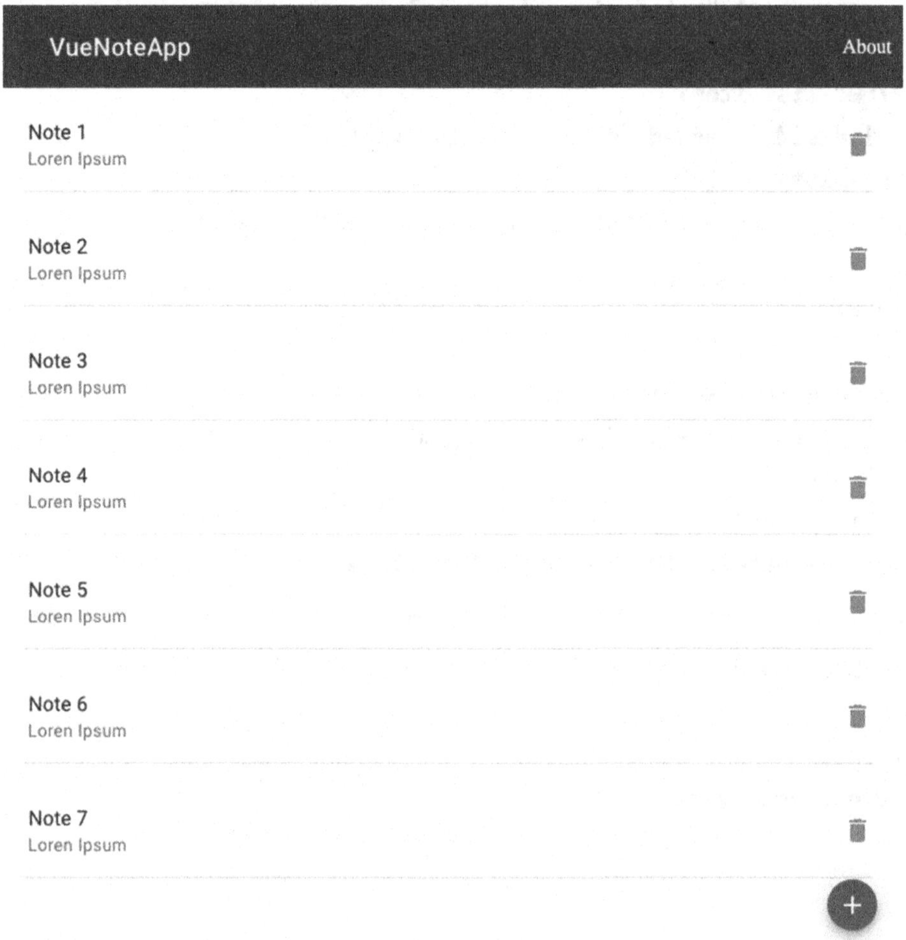

Figure 9-20. *Adding* notesData *in* Dashboard.vue

Users can make mistakes when inserting new notes. That is why we must allow them to delete notes. To accomplish this, we must modify our array and remove the element. JavaScript has a method that can help us with this: Splice. The Splice method allows us to change the content in our array.

We are going to create the handleDelete(id) method and add it to the Delete button, to which we are going to pass the item index that we want to delete. Using Splice, we can remove content from our Array, as shown in Listing 9-30.

Listing 9-30. DummyData Module

```
<!-- eslint-disable vue/no-deprecated-slot-attribute -->
<template>
  <div>
    <mwc-list v-for="(note) in notes" :key="note.id" multi>
      <mwc-list-item twoline hasMeta>
        <span>{{note.title}}</span>
        <span slot="meta" class="material-icons" @click="handleDelete
        (note.id)">delete</span>
        <span slot="secondary">{{note.description}}</span>
      </mwc-list-item>
      <li divider padded role="separator"></li>
    </mwc-list>
    <mwc-fab class="floatButton" mini icon="add"></mwc-fab>
  </div>
</template>
<script>
import '@material/mwc-list/mwc-list';
import '@material/mwc-list/mwc-list-item';
import '@material/mwc-fab';
import '@material/mwc-button';
import { notesData } from '../utils/DummyData';

export default {
  name: 'Dashboard',
  data() {
    return {
      notes: notesData
```

```
    }
  },
  methods: {
    handleDelete(id) {
      const noteToDelete = this.notes.findIndex((item) => (item.id ===
      id));
      this.notes.splice(noteToDelete, 1);
    }
  },
}
</script>
<style scoped>
  .floatButton {
    position: fixed;
    bottom: 20px;
    right: 20px;
  }
</style>
```

You can access the relevant code from the GitHub repository at `$git checkout v1.0.5`.

Adding New Notes

At this point, we can load our notes dynamically, and we can delete notes from our list. Now we are going to add a mechanism to add new notes, using the `fab` button that we added previously at the bottom-right corner. To achieve this, we are going to use `mwc-dialog`, to show a modal with a form with which the user can add new notes or cancel and return to the list of notes (see Figure 9-21).

Figure 9-21. *mwc-dialog in Dashboard.vue*

Also, we are going to add the library uuid. With this library, we can generate new unique ids for the new notes. Run the following:

```
$npm install -save uuid
```

In the template, we are going to add mwc-dialog, as in Listing 9-31.

Listing 9-31. Adding mwc-dialog

```
<!-- eslint-disable vue/no-deprecated-slot-attribute -->
<template>
  <div>
    <mwc-list v-for="(note) in notes" :key="note.id" multi>
      <mwc-list-item twoline hasMeta>
        <span>{{note.title}}</span>
        <span slot="meta" class="material-icons" @click="handleDelete
        (note.id)">delete</span>
        <span slot="secondary">{{note.description}}</span>
      </mwc-list-item>
      <li divider padded role="separator"></li>
    </mwc-list>
```

```
<mwc-fab class="floatButton" @click="handleAdd" mini icon="add">
</mwc-fab>
<mwc-dialog id="dialog" heading="Add Note">
  <div class="formFields">
    <mwc-textfield
      id="text-title"
      outlined
      minlength="3"
      label="Title"
      required>
    </mwc-textfield>
  </div>
  <div class="formFields">
  <mwc-textfield
    id="text-description"
    outlined
    minlength="3"
    label="Description"
    required>
  </mwc-textfield>
  </div>
  <div>
  <mwc-button
    id="primary-action-button"
    slot="primaryAction"
    @click="handleAddNote">
    Add
  </mwc-button>
  <mwc-button
    slot="secondaryAction"
    dialogAction="close"
    @click="handleClose">
    Cancel
  </mwc-button>
  </div>
```

```
    </mwc-dialog>
  </div>
</template>
```

Here, we are adding a form inside `mwc-dialog` that uses `mwc-textfield` and `mwc-button` components to allow the new note to enter and trigger the `handleAddNote` method or the `handleClose` method to handle what the user selects. Next, we are going to add this logic in `Dashboard.vue`, as in Listing 9-32.

Listing 9-32. Adding `mwc-dialog`

```
<!-- eslint-disable vue/no-deprecated-slot-attribute -->
<template>
  <div>
    <mwc-list v-for="(note) in notes" :key="note.id" multi>
      <mwc-list-item twoline hasMeta>
        <span>{{note.title}}</span>
        <span slot="meta" class="material-icons" @click="handleDelete
        (note.id)">delete</span>
        <span slot="secondary">{{note.description}}</span>
      </mwc-list-item>
      <li divider padded role="separator"></li>
    </mwc-list>
    <mwc-fab class="floatButton" @click="handleAdd" mini icon="add">
    </mwc-fab>
    <mwc-dialog id="dialog" heading="Add Note">
      <div class="formFields">
        <mwc-textfield
          id="text-title"
          outlined
          minlength="3"
          label="Title"
          required>
        </mwc-textfield>
      </div>
      <div class="formFields">
      <mwc-textfield
```

175

```
          id="text-description"
          outlined
          minlength="3"
          label="Description"
          required>
      </mwc-textfield>
      </div>
      <div>
      <mwc-button
        id="primary-action-button"
        slot="primaryAction"
        @click="handleAddNote">
        Add
      </mwc-button>
      <mwc-button
        slot="secondaryAction"
        dialogAction="close"
        @click="handleClose">
        Cancel
      </mwc-button>
      </div>
    </mwc-dialog>
  </div>
</template>
<script>
import '@material/mwc-list/mwc-list';
import '@material/mwc-list/mwc-list-item';
import '@material/mwc-fab';
import '@material/mwc-button';
import '@material/mwc-dialog';
import '@material/mwc-textfield';
import { notesData } from '../utils/DummyData';
import { v4 as uuidv4 } from 'uuid';
```

```
export default {
  name: 'Dashboard',
  data() {
    return {
      notes: notesData
    }
  },
  methods: {
    handleDelete(id) {
      const noteToDelete = this.notes.findIndex((item) => (item.id === id));
      this.notes.splice(noteToDelete, 1);
    },
    handleAdd() {
      const formDialog = this.$el.querySelector('#dialog');
      formDialog.show();
    },
    handleAddNote() {
      const formDialog = this.$el.querySelector('#dialog');
      let txtTitle = this.$el.querySelector('#text-title');
      let txtDescription = this.$el.querySelector('#text-description');
      const isValid = txtTitle.checkValidity() && txtDescription.
      checkValidity();

      if(isValid) {
        const newIndex = uuidv4();
        this.notes.push({id: newIndex, title: txtTitle.value, description:
        txtDescription.value});

        txtTitle.value ='';
        txtDescription.value = '';
        formDialog.close();
      }
    },
```

```
    handleClose() {
      let txtTitle = this.$el.querySelector('#text-title');
      let txtDescription = this.$el.querySelector('#text-description');
      const formDialog = this.$el.querySelector('#dialog');

      txtTitle.value ='';
      txtDescription.value = '';
      formDialog.close();
    }
  },
}
</script>
<style scoped>
  .floatButton {
    position: fixed;
    bottom: 20px;
    right: 20px;
  }

  .formFields {
    margin: 15px;
  }
</style>
```

Here, we are using this.$el.querySelector() to select the web components and use their methods to execute logic, such as, for example, formDialog.show() and formDialog. close(), to show and hide the mwc-dialog. Also, in handleAddNote(), we are using the uuidv4() method to generate a new index with the data that the user enters in the form and, with this.notes.push(), add the new note in the local array that we are using to keep all our notes. With these modifications, you can add notes (see Figure 9-22).

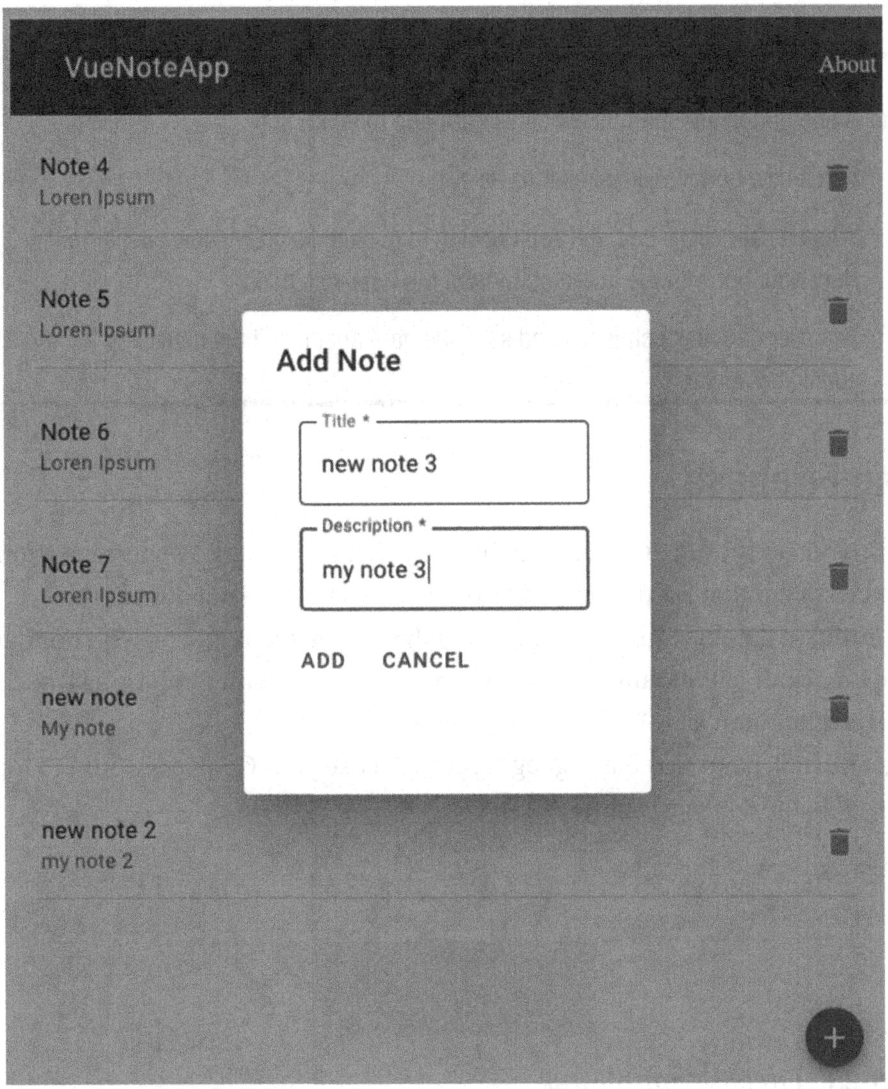

Figure 9-22. *Adding new notes*

You can access the relevant code from the GitHub repository at `$git checkout v1.0.6`.

Adding Firebase

If you try to reload the app, you can see that we lost all our notes. We need an external persistence system that keeps our data and syncs this between all our clients.

The Firebase database gives us a perfect solution for keeping sync with our data in real time for all our clients, and we can save the data easily with Firebase's JavaScript software development kit (SDK).

To get started, go to firebase.google.com and use your Google account to log in. Next, go to the console (Figure 9-23).

Figure 9-23. *Firebase console link*

Create a new project (Figure 9-24).

Figure 9-24. *Adding the Project button*

Next, you are going to choose the name of your project (Figure 9-25).

Figure 9-25. *Creating a new project in Firebase*

Choose whether you want to use Google Analytics integration in your project (Figure 9-26).

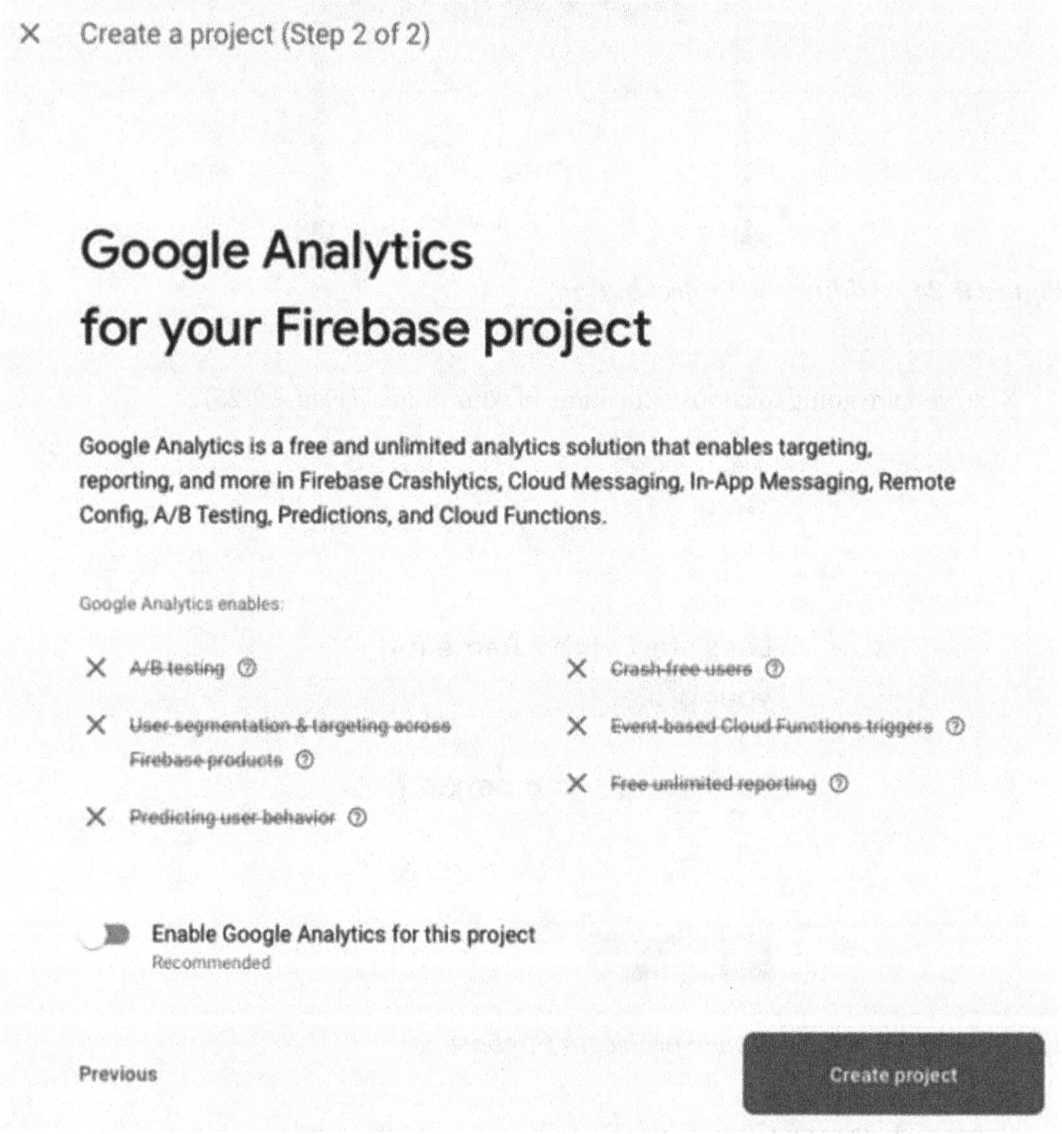

X   Create a project (Step 2 of 2)

Google Analytics for your Firebase project

Google Analytics is a free and unlimited analytics solution that enables targeting, reporting, and more in Firebase Crashlytics, Cloud Messaging, In-App Messaging, Remote Config, A/B Testing, Predictions, and Cloud Functions.

Google Analytics enables:

X A/B testing ⑦

X User segmentation & targeting across Firebase products ⑦

X Predicting user behavior ⑦

X Crash-free users ⑦

X Event-based Cloud Functions triggers ⑦

X Free unlimited reporting ⑦

▣ **Enable Google Analytics for this project**
Recommended

Previous   Create project

Figure 9-26. *Adding Google Analytics to the new Firebase project*

In just minutes, you can start to use your new project.

When your project is ready in the Firebase console, you are going to require some information that allows you to connect our app and Firebase.

For this, go to Project Overview ➤ Project settings. (See Figure 9-27.)

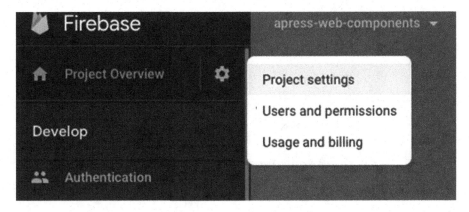

Figure 9-27. *Firebase Project Overview*

Now click the web app icon (Figure 9-28).

Figure 9-28. *Firebase project settings view*

Firebase is going to start a wizard (Figure 9-29).

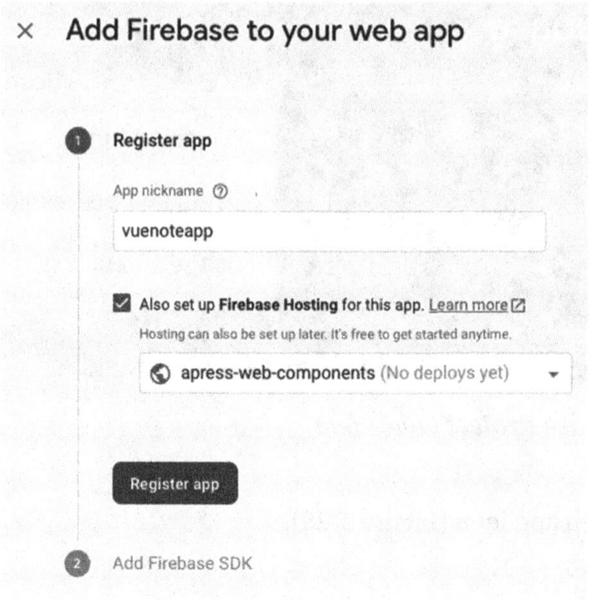
Add Firebase to your web app
Register app
App nickname
vuenoteapp
Also set up Firebase Hosting for this app. Learn more
Hosting can also be set up later. It's free to get started anytime.
apress-web-components (No deploys yet)
Register app
Add Firebase SDK

Figure 9-29. *Firebase web app wizard*

At the end, you will see our `firebaseConfig` summary (Figure 9-30).

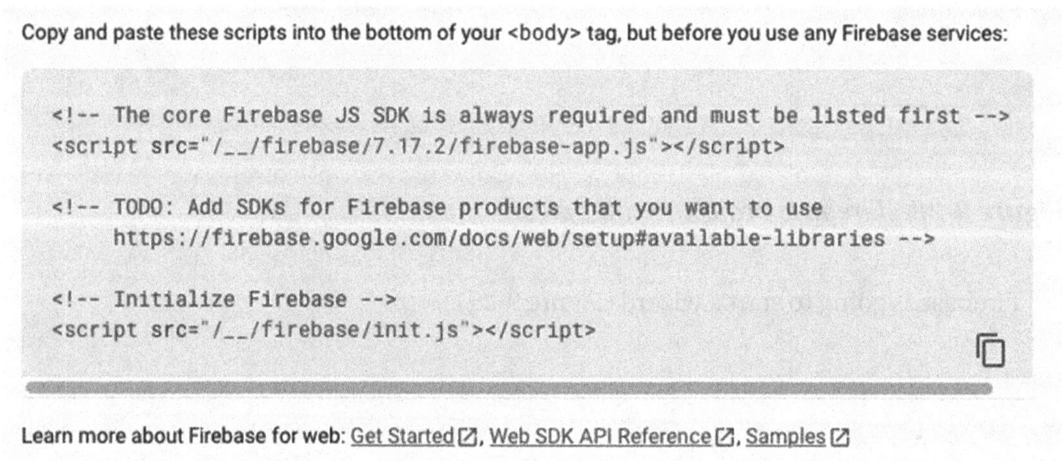
Copy and paste these scripts into the bottom of your <body> tag, but before you use any Firebase services:
<!-- The core Firebase JS SDK is always required and must be listed first -->
<script src="/__/firebase/7.17.2/firebase-app.js"></script>
<!-- TODO: Add SDKs for Firebase products that you want to use
https://firebase.google.com/docs/web/setup#available-libraries -->
<!-- Initialize Firebase -->
<script src="/__/firebase/init.js"></script>
Learn more about Firebase for web: Get Started, Web SDK API Reference, Samples

Figure 9-30. *Firebase configuration summary*

Copy this information. You will need it when we create the `firebase.js` file for our project.

The last thing that we need to make in the console is a new database and the security rules to access it without authentication. (We do this to keep our app simple.)

Go to Database (Figure 9-31).

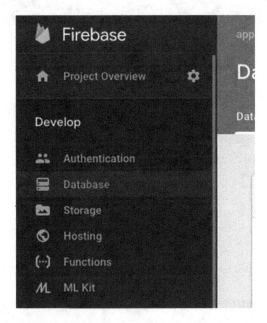

Figure 9-31. *Firebase Database link*

Select Create Realtime Database (Figure 9-32).

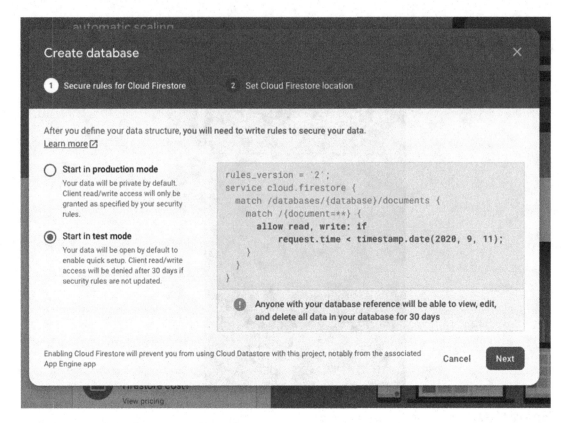

Figure 9-32. *Firebase security rules*

Select Start in test mode. In this mode, we can write data in our database without having authentication. This is handy in development but unsafe in production. Now we can go back to our app.

In the terminal run the following:

```
$npm install firebase --save
```

Create a new `firebase.js` file and paste the data from your Firebase Project, as in Listing 9-33.

Listing 9-33. Adding Firebase

```
import Firebase from 'firebase';

let config = {
  apiKey: "xxx",
```

```
    authDomain: "xxx",
    databaseURL: "xxx",
    projectId: "xxx",
    storageBucket: "xxx",
    messagingSenderId: "xxx",
    appId: "xxx"
};

Firebase.initializeApp(config)

export const fireApp = Firebase;
```

Import `main.js`, as shown in Listing 9-34.

Listing 9-34. Importing Firebase in `main.js`

```
import Firebase from 'firebase';

import './firebase';
import { createApp } from 'vue'
import App from './App.vue'
import router from './router'

createApp(App).use(router).mount('#app')...
```

You can access the relevant code from the GitHub repository at `$git checkout v1.0.7`.

Now, in `Dashboard.vue`, we must use the life cycle `mounted()` method and recover all the notes in our real-time database. We must also update `saveNote()` and `deleteNote()`, to update the new notes in Firebase.

With the following, we import Fireapp from `firebase.js` to keep a reference in our app:

```
const db = fireApp.database().ref();
```

Now, with `db.push`, we add data to Firebase, and with `remove()`, we can delete data from Firebase (Listing 9-35). For additional information, you can access the relevant documents at `https://firebase.google.com/docs/reference/js/firebase.database`.

Listing 9-35. Adding Firebase in `Dashboard.vue`

```
<!-- eslint-disable vue/no-deprecated-slot-attribute -->
<template>
  <div>
    <mwc-list v-for="(note) in notes" :key="note.id" multi>
      <mwc-list-item twoline hasMeta>
        <span>{{note.title}}</span>
        <span slot="meta" class="material-icons" @click="handleDelete
        (note.id)">delete</span>
        <span slot="secondary">{{note.description}}</span>
      </mwc-list-item>
      <li divider padded role="separator"></li>
    </mwc-list>
    <mwc-fab class="floatButton" @click="handleAdd" mini icon="add">
    </mwc-fab>
    <mwc-dialog id="dialog" heading="Add Note">
      <div class="formFields">
        <mwc-textfield
          id="text-title"
          outlined
          minlength="3"
          label="Title"
          required>
        </mwc-textfield>
      </div>
      <div class="formFields">
        <mwc-textfield
          id="text-description"
          outlined
          minlength="3"
          label="Description"
          required>
        </mwc-textfield>
      </div>
```

```
    <div>
      <mwc-button
        id="primary-action-button"
        slot="primaryAction"
        @click="handleAddNote">
        Add
      </mwc-button>
      <mwc-button
        slot="secondaryAction"
        dialogAction="close"
        @click="handleClose">
        Cancel
      </mwc-button>
    </div>
  </mwc-dialog>
  </div>
</template>
<script>
import '@material/mwc-list/mwc-list';
import '@material/mwc-list/mwc-list-item';
import '@material/mwc-fab';
import '@material/mwc-button';
import '@material/mwc-dialog';
import '@material/mwc-textfield';
import { fireApp } from'../firebase'
import { v4 as uuidv4 } from 'uuid';

const db = fireApp.database().ref();

export default {
  name: 'Dashboard',
  data() {
    return {
      notes: []
    }
  },
```

```
mounted() {
  db.once('value', (notes) => {
    notes.forEach((note) => {
      this.notes.push({
        id: note.child('id').val(),
        title: note.child('title').val(),
        description: note.child('description').val(),
        ref: note.ref
      })
    })
  });
},
methods: {
  handleDelete(id) {
    const noteToDelete = this.notes.findIndex((item) => (item.id === id));
    const noteRef = this.notes[noteToDelete].ref;
    if(noteRef) {
      noteRef.remove();
    }
    this.notes.splice(noteToDelete, 1);
  },
  handleAdd() {
    const formDialog = this.$el.querySelector('#dialog');
    formDialog.show();
  },
  handleAddNote() {
    const formDialog = this.$el.querySelector('#dialog');
    let txtTitle = this.$el.querySelector('#text-title');
    let txtDescription = this.$el.querySelector('#text-description');
    const isValid = txtTitle.checkValidity() && txtDescription.
    checkValidity();

    if(isValid) {
      const newIndex = uuidv4();
      const newItem = {id: newIndex, title: txtTitle.value, description:
      txtDescription.value};
```

```
        this.notes.push(newItem);
        db.push(newItem);

        txtTitle.value ='';
        txtDescription.value = '';
        formDialog.close();
      }
    },
    handleClose() {
      let txtTitle = this.$el.querySelector('#text-title');
      let txtDescription = this.$el.querySelector('#text-description');
      const formDialog = this.$el.querySelector('#dialog');

      txtTitle.value ='';
      txtDescription.value = '';
      formDialog.close();
    }
  },
}
</script>
<style scoped>
  .floatButton {
    position: fixed;
    bottom: 20px;
    right: 20px;
  }

  .formFields {
    margin: 15px;
  }
</style>
```

Now we can see our data store in Firebase (Figure 9-33).

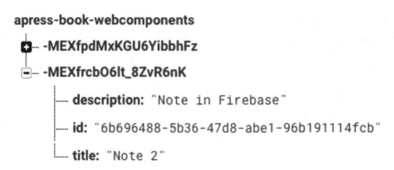

apress-book-webcomponents

⊟⋯ **-MEXfpdMxKGU6YibbhFz**

⊟⋯ **-MEXfrcbO6lt_8ZvR6nK**

├──── **description:** "Note in Firebase"

├──── **id:** "6b696488-5b36-47d8-abe1-96b191114fcb"

└──── **title:** "Note 2"

Figure 9-33. *Firebase database console*

When we refresh, our data will be saved (Figure 9-34).

VueNoteApp   About

Note 1
Note in Firebase   🗑

Note 2
Note in Firebase   🗑

⊕

Figure 9-34. *VueNoteApp with persistence in Firebase*

You can access the relevant code from the GitHub repository at `$git checkout chap-9`.

Summary

In this chapter, you learned the following:

- Vue.js is focused on the view layer only and is easy to pick up and integrate with other libraries or existing projects.

- Components are created and destroyed in processes known collectively as the life cycle. There are some methods we can use to run functions in specific moments. These methods are called life cycle hooks. Life cycle hooks are an essential part of any serious component.

- Components usually need to share information between them. For these basic scenarios, we can use props, the ref attribute, emitters, and two-way data binding.

- Vue Router is an official routing plug-in for single-page applications designed for use within the Vue.js framework. A router is a way to jump from one view to another in a single-page application.

- We can use the Firebase database to keep our notes synced among all the clients.

CHAPTER 10

Publishing

Congratulations! We now have our web app, using Vue.js and Web Components, but we want to share our app with the world. Firebase Hosting can help us to make our app public, and Firebase Authentication allows us to add an authentication system and register users and associated notes to each one.

Adding Firebase Authentication

Through its software development kit, Firebase Authentication gives us a secure method by which to add authentication in our JavaScript app. We must, however, choose the sign-in providers that we are going to support in our app. You can choose between the most popular, such as Facebook and Google, or integrate sign-in into a custom authentication system. We are going to choose only email and a password, to keep things simple.

First, we are going to go to the Firebase web console and select Authentication (see Figure 10-1).

Figure 10-1. *Authentication link in Firebase web console*

© Carlos Rojas 2021
C. Rojas, *Building Native Web Components*, https://doi.org/10.1007/978-1-4842-5905-4_10

In Authentication (Figure 10-2), we are going to select Sign-in method.

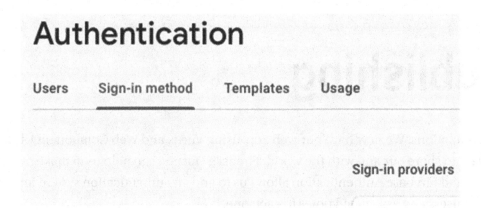

Figure 10-2. *Authentication section in Firebase web console*

Now enable Email/Password (Figure 10-3).

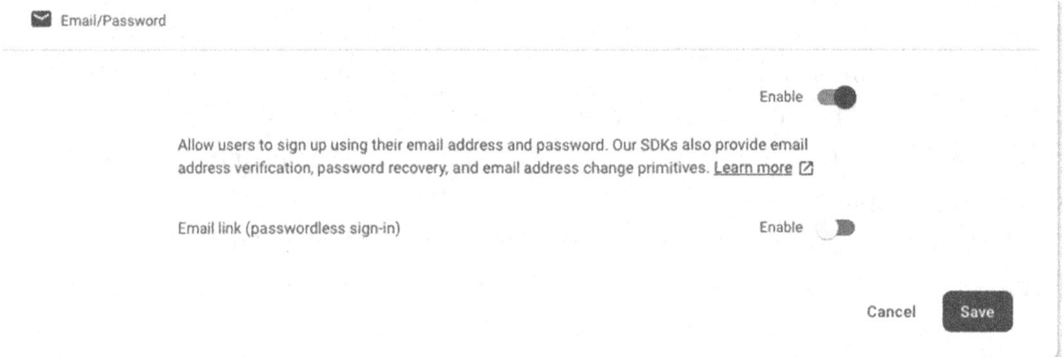

Figure 10-3. *Enabling Email/Password authentication in the Firebase web console*

OK, that's all for the web console for now.

Back to our code. We require a new component with a form with which we can enter an email and password, to execute the authentication process.

Create a new components/Login.vue file and add a template, as in Listing 10-1.

Listing 10-1. Adding a Template in Login.vue

```
<!-- eslint-disable vue/no-deprecated-slot-attribute -->
<template>
  <div class="formContainer">
    <div class="formLogin">
      <div class="formFields">
        <h1>{{actionText}}</h1>
        <mwc-textfield
            id="text-email"
            outlined
            minlength="3"
            label="Email"
            required>
          </mwc-textfield>
        </div>
        <div class="formFields">
          <mwc-textfield
            id="text-password"
            type="password"
            outlined
            minlength="3"
            label="Password"
            required>
          </mwc-textfield>
        </div>
        <div class="actionButtons">
          <mwc-button
            id="link-action-button"
            class="actionButton"
            slot="primaryAction"
            @click="goToLink">
            {{linkButton}}
          </mwc-button>
        </div>
```

```
        <div class="actionButtons">
          <mwc-button
            raised
            id="primary-action-button"
            class="actionButton"
            slot="primaryAction"
            @click="submitAction">
            {{actionButton}}
          </mwc-button>
          <mwc-button
            raised
            slot="secondary-action-button"
            class="actionButton"
            @click="handleClear">
            Clear
          </mwc-button>
        </div>
      </div>
    </div>
</template>
<script>
import '@material/mwc-textfield';
import '@material/mwc-button';
export default {
  name: 'Login',
  data() {
    return {
      actionText: 'Login',
      actionButton: 'Send',
      linkButton: 'Register'
    }
  },
  methods: {
    goToLink () {
      switch(this.linkButton) {
```

```
      case 'Login':
        this.actionText= 'Login';
        this.actionButton= 'Send';
        this.linkButton = 'Register';
        break;
      case 'Register':
        this.actionText= 'Register';
        this.actionButton= 'Register';
        this.linkButton = 'Login';
        break;
      }
    },

}
</script>
<style scoped>
  .formContainer {
    display:flex;
  }

  .formLogin {
    margin:auto;
  }

  .formFields {
    margin: 15px;
  }

  .actionButtons {
    text-align:center;
  }

  .actionButton {
    margin: 10px;
  }
</style>
```

With this, we are adding a form to Login and Register users. We are using the same view for both operations and `actionText`, `actionButton`, and `linkButton` to switch the texts that the user can see in the view, as shown in Figure 10-4.

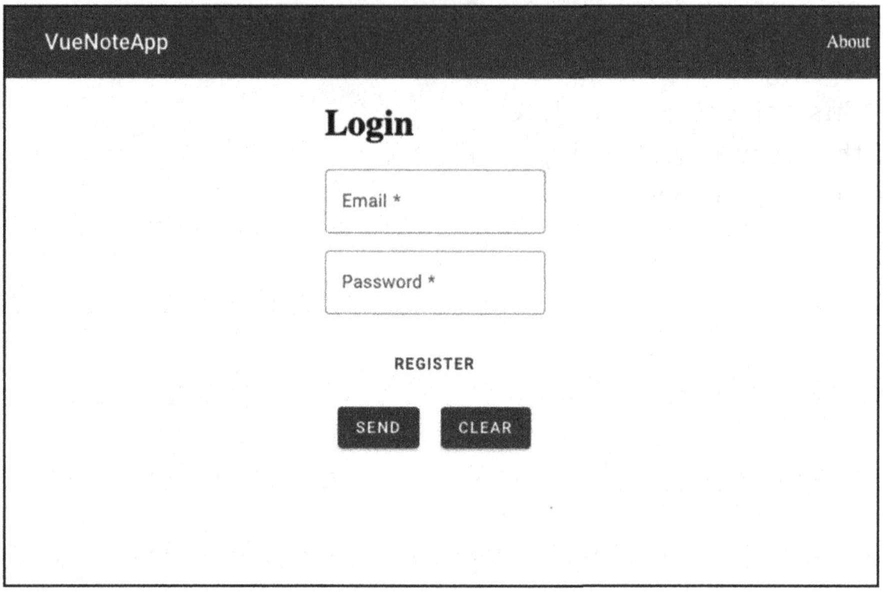

Figure 10-4. *Login component*

The next step is to add the authentication features (Listing 10-2).

Listing 10-2. Adding a Firebase Authentication in `Login.vue`

```
<!-- eslint-disable vue/no-deprecated-slot-attribute -->
<template>
  <div class="formContainer">
    <div class="formLogin">
      <div class="formFields">
        <h1>{{actionText}}</h1>
        <mwc-textfield
            id="text-email"
            outlined
            minlength="3"
```

```
      label="Email"
      required>
    </mwc-textfield>
  </div>
  <div class="formFields">
    <mwc-textfield
      id="text-password"
      type="password"
      outlined
      minlength="3"
      label="Password"
      required>
    </mwc-textfield>
  </div>
  <div class="actionButtons">
    <mwc-button
      id="link-action-button"
      class="actionButton"
      slot="primaryAction"
      @click="goToLink">
      {{linkButton}}
    </mwc-button>
  </div>
  <div class="actionButtons">
    <mwc-button
      raised
      id="primary-action-button"
      class="actionButton"
      slot="primaryAction"
      @click="submitAction">
      {{actionButton}}
    </mwc-button>
    <mwc-button
      raised
      slot="secondary-action-button"
```

```
              class="actionButton"
              @click="handleClear">
              Clear
          </mwc-button>
        </div>
      </div>
  </div>
</template>
<script>
import '@material/mwc-textfield';
import '@material/mwc-button';
import { fireApp } from '../firebase';

const auth = fireApp.auth();

export default {
  name: 'Login',
  data() {
    return {
      actionText: 'Login',
      actionButton: 'Send',
      linkButton: 'Register'
    }
  },
  methods: {
    goToLink () {
      switch(this.linkButton) {
      case 'Login':
        this.actionText= 'Login';
        this.actionButton= 'Send';
        this.linkButton = 'Register';
        break;
      case 'Register':
        this.actionText= 'Register';
        this.actionButton= 'Register';
        this.linkButton = 'Login';
```

```
    break;
  }
},
goToDashboard () {
  this.$router.push('/dashboard');
},
signInUser (email, password) {
  auth.signInWithEmailAndPassword(email,password)
  .then(
    () => {
    this.goToDashboard();
    }
  )
  .catch(
    // eslint-disable-next-line
    (error) => {console.log('Something happened.', error)}
  );
},
signUpUser (email, password) {
  auth.createUserWithEmailAndPassword(email,password)
  .then(
    // eslint-disable-next-line
    (user) => {console.log('User registered.', user)}
  )
  .catch(
    // eslint-disable-next-line
    (error) => {console.log('Something happened.', error)}
  );
},
submitAction () {

  let txtEmail = this.$el.querySelector('#text-email');
  let txtPassword = this.$el.querySelector('#text-password');
  const isValid = txtEmail.checkValidity() && txtPassword.
  checkValidity();
```

```
      if(isValid) {
        switch(this.actionText) {
          case 'Login':
            this.signInUser (txtEmail.value, txtPassword.value);

            txtEmail.value = '';
            txtPassword.value ='';
            break;
          case 'Register':
            this.signUpUser (txtEmail.value, txtPassword.value);

            txtEmail.value = '';
            txtPassword.value ='';
            break;
      }
      }
    }
  },
}
</script>
<style scoped>
  .formContainer {
    display:flex;
  }

  .formLogin {
    margin:auto;
  }

  .formFields {
    margin: 15px;
  }

  .actionButtons {
    text-align:center;
  }
```

```
.actionButton {
  margin: 10px;
}
</style>
```

Here, we are using the submitAction() method to check if we are creating a new user or login in the app and passing the email and the password that the user enters in the form. If the user wants to log in to the app, we use the Firebase auth. signInWithEmailAndPassword() method to check if the user exists in Firebase. If the password is correct, we are redirected to the Dashboard view. If the user is creating a new account, we use the Firebase auth.createUserWithEmailAndPassword() method to add this new user to Firebase.

Finally, we are going to modify our file router/index.js to add this new component (Listing 10-3).

Listing 10-3. Adding the Login Component in the Vue Router

```
<!-- eslint-disable vue/no-deprecated-slot-attribute -->
import { createRouter, createWebHistory } from 'vue-router'
import Login from '../views/Login.vue'

const routes = [
  {
    path: '',
    component: Login
  },
  {
    path: '/login',
    name: 'Login',
    component: Login
  },
  {
    path: '/dashboard',
    name: 'Dashboard',
    component: () => import(/* webpackChunkName: "dashboard" */ '../views/
    Dashboard.vue')
  },
```

```
  {
    path: '/about',
    name: 'About',
    component: () => import(/* webpackChunkName: "about" */ '../views/
    About.vue')
  }
]

const router = createRouter({
  history: createWebHistory(process.env.BASE_URL),
  routes
})
export default router
```

From the GitHub repository (https://github.com/carlosrojaso/apress-book-web-components), you can access the relevant code at $git checkout v1.0.8.

Adding Guards

Now, in App.vue, we must add a mechanism to prevent users not logged in from accessing Dashboard.vue directly from the URL. To achieve this, we are going to use a feature from Vue Router called Guards. Guards are primarily used to guard navigations, either by redirecting or canceling them. You can learn more about Guards at https://router.vuejs.org/guide/advanced/navigation-guards.html#global-before-guards. We are going to add this mechanism in our router/index.js file (Listing 10-4).

Listing 10-4. Adding Navigation Guards in the Vue Router

```
import { createRouter, createWebHistory } from 'vue-router'
import Login from '../views/Login.vue'
import { fireApp } from '../firebase';

const routes = [
  {
    path: '',
    component: Login
  },
```

```
  {
    path: '/login',
    name: 'Login',
    component: Login
  },
  {
    path: '/dashboard',
    name: 'Dashboard',
    component: () => import(/* webpackChunkName: "dashboard" */ '../views/
    Dashboard.vue'),
    meta: {
      requiresAuth: true
    }
  },
  {
    path: '/about',
    name: 'About',
    component: () => import(/* webpackChunkName: "about" */ '../views/
    About.vue')
  }
]

const router = createRouter({
  history: createWebHistory(process.env.BASE_URL),
  routes
})

router.beforeEach(async (to, from, next) => {
  const requiresAuth = to.matched.some(record => record.meta.requiresAuth);
  if (requiresAuth && !await fireApp.getCurrentUser()) {
    next('Login');
  } else {
    next();
  }
})

export default router
```

Here, we are using a route meta field in /Dashboard to enforce the authentication in this route, and we are checking this in the guard. Also, we are checking for the getCurrentUser() method from fireApp. We must add this method in firebase.js (Listing 10-5).

Listing 10-5. Adding the getCurrentUser() Method in firebase.js

```
import Firebase from 'firebase';

let config = {
  apiKey: "xxx",
  authDomain: "xxx",
  databaseURL: "xxx",
  projectId: "xxx",
  storageBucket: "xxx",
  messagingSenderId: "xxx",
  appId: "xxx"
};

Firebase.initializeApp(config)

Firebase.getCurrentUser = () => {
  return new Promise((resolve, reject) => {
      const unsubscribe = Firebase.auth().onAuthStateChanged(user => {
          unsubscribe();
          resolve(user);
      }, reject);
  })
};
export const fireApp = Firebase;
```

The getCurrentUser method gives us information about the current user or a rejection. Finally, we are going to add a logout link at the top, for users to close their sessions.

In App.vue, we are going to add a link in <mwc-top-app-bar> (Listing 10-6).

Listing 10-6. Adding Logout Mechanism in `App.vue`

```
<!-- eslint-disable vue/no-deprecated-slot-attribute -->
<template>
  <mwc-top-app-bar>
    <div slot="title"><router-link to="/">VueNoteApp</router-link></div>
    <div slot="actionItems"><router-link to="/About">About</router-link>
    </div>
    <div slot="actionItems" v-if="logged" @click="handleLogout">Logout
    </div>
    <div><router-view/></div>
  </mwc-top-app-bar>
</template>

<script>
import '@material/mwc-top-app-bar';

import { fireApp } from './firebase';
const auth = fireApp.auth();

export default {
  name: 'App',
  data() {
    return {
      logged: false
    }
  },
  mounted() {
    fireApp.getCurrentUser()
      .then((user)=> {
        this.logged = user;
        this.$router.push('Dashboard');
        })
      .catch(() => {
        this.logged = false;
      });
  },
```

```
  methods: {
    handleAbout() {
      this.$router.push('About');
    },
    handleLogout() {
      auth.signOut()
        .then(()=>{
          this.$router.push('/login');
          this.logged= false;
          })
        .catch((error)=> {
          // eslint-disable-next-line
          console.log('error', error)
        });
    }
  },
}
</script>

<style>
  a, a:visited {
    color:white;
    text-decoration:none;
    padding: 5px;
  }
</style>
```

Here, we are using fireApp.currentUser() to check if the user is logged in when Login.vue is mounted(), if we can jump directly to Dashboard.vue, or if we require that the user enter credentials. Also, we create handleLogout(), a method that uses auth. signOut to close the session and redirect the user to Login.vue. When the user is logged in, we show the logout link, using the v-if directive, Then, only when the user has already logged in, we show this link to the user (Figure 10-5).

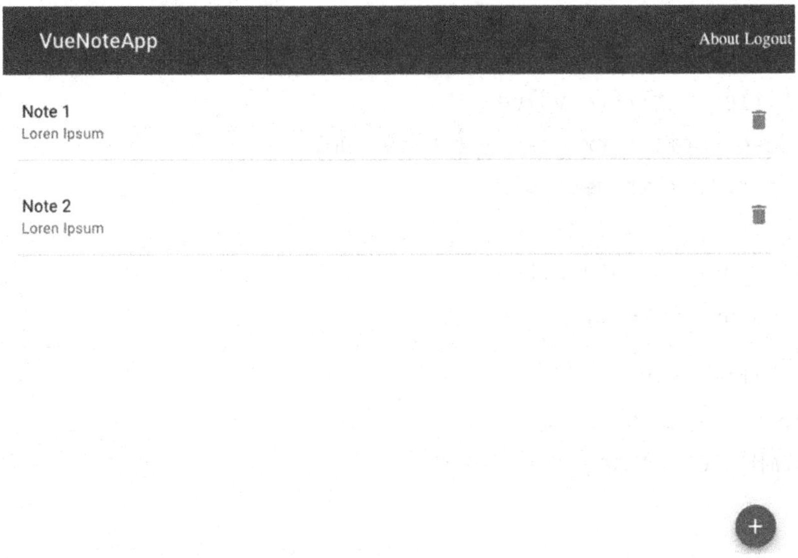

Figure 10-5. *Logout link*

From the GitHub repository (`https://github.com/carlosrojaso/apress-book-web-components`), you can access the relevant code at`$git checkout v1.0.9`.

Adding a User to Data

If you create several users and add or delete notes, you can see that these notes are shared in all the accounts. This happens because we are not filtering the notes for each user. To achieve this, we must take some extra steps.

First, we are going to add the user ID in each note that a user creates, as in Listing 10-7.

Listing 10-7. Adding `userId` Property in New Notes

```
...
    handleAddNote() {
        const formDialog = this.$el.querySelector('#dialog');
        let txtTitle = this.$el.querySelector('#text-title');
        let txtDescription = this.$el.querySelector('#text-description');
        const isValid = txtTitle.checkValidity() && txtDescription.
        checkValidity();
        if(isValid) {
            const newIndex = uuidv4();
```

```
    const newItem = {
      id: newIndex,
      title: txtTitle.value,
      description: txtDescription.value,
      userId: this.user.uid
    };
    this.notes.push(newItem);
    db.push(newItem);

    txtTitle.value ='';
    txtDescription.value = '';
    formDialog.close();
  }
},
...
```

Now the data have a relationship between each note and the user that created that note (Figure 10-6).

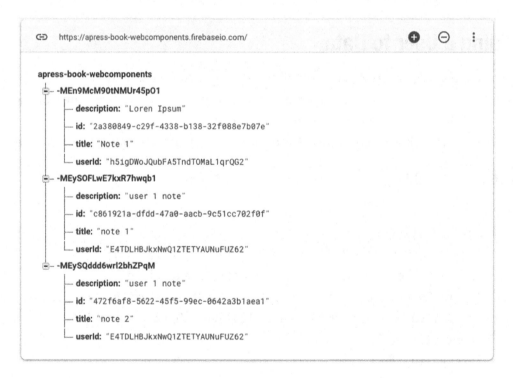

Figure 10-6. *Firebase web console database data*

Now we must return to the Firebase web console and update our security rules (Figure 10-7).

```
1 ▾  {
2 ▾    "rules": {
3        ".indexOn": "userId",
4        ".read": "auth !== null",
5        ".write": "auth !== null"
6      }
7    }
```

Figure 10-7. *Firebase web console database security rules*

With this, only logged-in sessions can read and write data in our database. In addition, we create an index with userId, to perform search/sorts faster.

Now we must filter the notes (Listing 10-8).

Listing 10-8. Adding a Login in the Vue Router

```
<!-- eslint-disable vue/no-deprecated-slot-attribute -->
<template>
  <div>
    <mwc-list v-for="(note) in notes" :key="note.id" multi>
      <mwc-list-item twoline hasMeta>
        <span>{{note.title}}</span>
        <span slot="meta" class="material-icons" @click="handleDelete
        (note.id)">delete</span>
        <span slot="secondary">{{note.description}}</span>
      </mwc-list-item>
```

```
    <li divider padded role="separator"></li>
</mwc-list>
<mwc-fab class="floatButton" @click="handleAdd" mini icon="add">
</mwc-fab>
<mwc-dialog id="dialog" heading="Add Note">
  <div class="formFields">
    <mwc-textfield
      id="text-title"
      outlined
      minlength="3"
      label="Title"
      required>
    </mwc-textfield>
  </div>
  <div class="formFields">
    <mwc-textfield
      id="text-description"
      outlined
      minlength="3"
      label="Description"
      required>
    </mwc-textfield>
  </div>
  <div>
    <mwc-button
      id="primary-action-button"
      slot="primaryAction"
      @click="handleAddNote">
      Add
    </mwc-button>
    <mwc-button
      slot="secondaryAction"
      dialogAction="close"
      @click="handleClose">
      Cancel
```

```
            </mwc-button>
          </div>
        </mwc-dialog>
      </div>
</template>
<script>
import '@material/mwc-list/mwc-list';
import '@material/mwc-list/mwc-list-item';
import '@material/mwc-fab';
import '@material/mwc-button';
import '@material/mwc-dialog';
import '@material/mwc-textfield';
import { fireApp } from'../firebase'
import { v4 as uuidv4 } from 'uuid';

const db = fireApp.database().ref();
const auth = fireApp.auth();

export default {
  name: 'Dashboard',
  data() {
    return {
      notes: [],
      user: null
    }
  },
  mounted() {
    this.isUserLoggedIn()
    .then(
      (user) => {
        this.user = user;
        this.updateLogged();
        this.getUserNotes();
      }
    )
```

```
    .catch(
      () => {
        this.$router.push('/login');
      }
    )
    ;
  },
  methods: {
    getUserNotes() {
      db.orderByChild('userId')
        .equalTo(this.user.uid)
        .once("value")
        .then(
          (notes) => {
            notes.forEach((note) => {
              this.notes.push({
                id: note.child('id').val(),
                title: note.child('title').val(),
                description: note.child('description').val(),
                userId: note.child('userId').val(),
                ref: note.ref
              })
            })
          }
        );
    },
    handleDelete(id) {
      const noteToDelete = this.notes.findIndex((item) => (item.id === id));
      const noteRef = this.notes[noteToDelete].ref;
      if(noteRef) {
        noteRef.remove();
      }
      this.notes.splice(noteToDelete, 1);
    },
```

```
handleAdd() {
  const formDialog = this.$el.querySelector('#dialog');
  formDialog.show();
},
handleAddNote() {
  const formDialog = this.$el.querySelector('#dialog');
  let txtTitle = this.$el.querySelector('#text-title');
  let txtDescription = this.$el.querySelector('#text-description');
  const isValid = txtTitle.checkValidity() && txtDescription.
  checkValidity();

  if(isValid) {
    const newIndex = uuidv4();
    const newItem = {
      id: newIndex,
      title: txtTitle.value,
      description: txtDescription.value,
      userId: this.user.uid
    };
    this.notes.push(newItem);
    db.push(newItem);

    txtTitle.value ='';
    txtDescription.value = '';
    formDialog.close();
  }
},
handleClose() {
  let txtTitle = this.$el.querySelector('#text-title');
  let txtDescription = this.$el.querySelector('#text-description');
  const formDialog = this.$el.querySelector('#dialog');

  txtTitle.value ='';
  txtDescription.value = '';
  formDialog.close();
},
```

```
    updateLogged() {
      this.$emit("update-logged", true);
    },
    isUserLoggedIn () {
        return new Promise(
          (resolve, reject) => {
            auth.onAuthStateChanged(function(user) {
              if (user) {
                resolve(user);
              }
              else {
                reject(user);
              }
            })
          }
        )
        ;
    }
  },
}
</script>
<style scoped>
  .floatButton {
    position: fixed;
    bottom: 20px;
    right: 20px;
  }

  .formFields {
    margin: 15px;
  }
</style>
```

Here, in the getUserNotes() method, we are getting the notes associated to one user, with the user ID db.orderByChild('userId').equalTo(this.user.uid).once("value"). With this, we fix the problem with the notes, and users can have their own notes in each account.

218

From the GitHub repository (`https://github.com/carlosrojaso/apress-book-web-components`), you can access the relevant code at `$git checkout v1.0.10`.

Sending to Firebase Hosting

First , we must authenticate our Firebase CLI with our Firebase account. To do this run the following:

`$ firebase login`

After successful authentication, you can start to use the Firebase tool to connect your apps with Firebase. The next step is to create our production bundle. To do this run

`$ npm run build`

This command creates the `dist/` folder with all our app optimized.

Now we must run the Firebase CLI wizard to connect VueNoteApp with Firebase (Figure 10-8). Run

`$ firebase init`

```
carlosrojaso@Carloss-MacBook-Pro-2 note-app % firebase init

    ######## #### ######## ######## ########      ###       ######  ########
    ##        ##  ##    ##  ##    ##      ##      ## ##  ## ##      ##
    ######    ##  ########  ######   ########  ######### ######  ######
    ##        ##  ##  ##    ##  ##   ##        ##     ##  ##    ## ##
    ##       #### ##   ##   ######## ########  ##       ##   ######  ########

You're about to initialize a Firebase project in this directory:

  /Users/carlosrojaso/Projects/apress-book-web-components/note-app

? Which Firebase CLI features do you want to set up for this folder? Press Space to select features, then Enter to confirm your choices.
 o Database: Deploy Firebase Realtime Database Rules
 o Firestore: Deploy rules and create indexes for Firestore
 o Functions: Configure and deploy Cloud Functions
 )● Hosting: Configure and deploy Firebase Hosting sites
 o Storage: Deploy Cloud Storage security rules
 o Emulators: Set up local emulators for Firebase features
```

Figure 10-8. *Firebase CLI Select service to configure*

Select hosting (see Figure 10-9).

? **Which Firebase CLI features do you want to set up for this folder?** Press Spac

=== **Project Setup**

First, let's associate this project directory with a Firebase project.
You can create multiple project aliases by running **firebase use --add,**
but for now we'll just set up a default project.

? **Please select an option:** Use an existing project
? **Select a default Firebase project for this directory:**
  amp-html-ionbook (amp-html-ionbook)
  amp-html-vueclassroom (amp-html-vueclassroom)
  appress-book-pwa (appress-book-pwa)
› apress-book-webcomponents (apress-book-webcomponents)
  apress-web-components (apress-web-components)
  carlosrojas-dev (www-carlosrojas-dev)
  codelab-22299 (frontend-bootstrapping)

Figure 10-9. *Firebase CLI Select Firebase project setup*

Select the project that you created in firebase.google.com—in my case, apress-book-webcomponents (Figure 10-10).

```
=== Hosting Setup

Your public directory is the folder (relative to your project directory) that
will contain Hosting assets to be uploaded with firebase deploy. If you
have a build process for your assets, use your build's output directory.

? What do you want to use as your public directory? dist
? Configure as a single-page app (rewrite all urls to /index.html)? No
✓ Wrote dist/404.html
? File dist/index.html already exists. Overwrite? No
i Skipping write of dist/index.html

i Writing configuration info to firebase.json...
i Writing project information to .firebaserc...

✓ Firebase initialization complete!
```

Figure 10-10. *Firebase CLI Select public directory*

The public directory is dist/.

OK. With this, we are ready to send our app to Firebase Hosting. To do this, run the following:

```
$ npm run build
$ Firebase deploy
```

You are going to see the progress as it appears in Figure 10-11.

```
carlosrojaso@Carloss-MacBook-Pro-2 note-app % firebase deploy

=== Deploying to 'apress-book-webcomponents'...

i  deploying hosting
i  hosting[apress-book-webcomponents]: beginning deploy...
i  hosting[apress-book-webcomponents]: found 26 files in dist
✓  hosting[apress-book-webcomponents]: file upload complete
i  hosting[apress-book-webcomponents]: finalizing version...
✓  hosting[apress-book-webcomponents]: version finalized
i  hosting[apress-book-webcomponents]: releasing new version...
✓  hosting[apress-book-webcomponents]: release complete

✓  Deploy complete!

Project Console: https://console.firebase.google.com/project/apress-book-webcomponents/overview
Hosting URL: https://apress-book-webcomponents.web.app
```

Figure 10-11. *Firebase CLI deploying and getting public URL*

In the end, you get a Hosting URL. This is your web URL. You can try it now with `https://apress-book-webcomponents.web.app`.

Summary

In this chapter, you learned

- How to use navigation guards in VueNoteApp

- How to enable email/password authentication in Firebase

- How to associate data to a user's account

- How to prepare and send web apps to Firebase Hosting

Final Thoughts

If you have reached this point, congratulations! You now know how to build, design, and use Web Components in any existing web app.

If you have any comments or feedback, feel free to contact me at `iam@carlosrojas.dev`.

If you have an issue regarding the code, don't hesitate to query the GitHub repository for this book at `https://github.com/carlosrojaso/apress-book-web-components/issues`.

In addition, for updates, check the official repository for the code (`https://github.com/carlosrojaso/apress-book-web-components`) frequently.

See you later, and keep programming!

Index

223